THE KENTISI

NORTH FORELAND L.
SOUTH FORELAND LIGHTHOUSE
GOODWIN SANDS LIGHTSHIPS
DUNGENESS LIGHTHOUSES

The 1904 Dungeness lighthouse at night.
Photo: Margaret Barnes

Alan Major

Other books on Kent by Alan Major
A New Dictionary of Kent Dialect. Meresborough Books
Whose Buried Where in Kent. Meresborough Books
Hidden Kent. Countryside Books
Cherries in the Rise. S. B. Publications
Goldings, Napoleons amd Romneys. S. B. Publications

To the past and present members of the Trinity House Lighthouse Service who manned the lighthouses and lightships and endured isolation and all that the forces of nature could hurl against them in order to be of assistance to seafarers.

First published in 2000 by S. B. Publications,
c/o 19 Grove Road, Seaford, East Sussex BN25 1TP

ISBN 1 85770 199 2

Designed and typeset by CGB, Lewes
Printed by MFP Design & Print
Longford Trading Estate, Thomas Street,
Stretford, Manchester M32 0JT

CONTENTS

ACKNOWLEDGEMENTS

The author acknowledges with grateful thanks the generous assistance given to him in various ways in the preparation of this book by :
William Lapthorne, Broadstairs; Connie and Ronald Cloke, Littlestone; Margaret and Christopher Barnes, New Romney; Sylvia and Ken Oiller, Dungeness; Vera Allen (Oiller), Iwade; Bill and Beryl Kennett, Dungeness; Betty Downs, Folkestone; Eddie J Aldridge, Selling; Rita Rodwell, GEC-Marconi, Chelmsford; Steven A Judd, National Trust, Dover; Rosemary Kent, National Trust, Lamberhurst; Di Bailey, Tunbridge Wells; Andrew Buckworth, Sturry; Annette Heal and H L Cooper of the Trinity House Lighthouse Service, London; Janet Adamson, Archivist, Folkestone Central Library and Heritage Service officers of Dover, Canterbury and Broadstairs public libraries.

Lastly, but by no means least, grateful thanks to Gerry Douglas-Sherwood of the Association of Lighthouse Keepers and to Tony Lane, editor of the association's magazine, *Lamp,* for their assistance and advice and for kindly checking the parts of the manuscript relevant to their experience.

PICTURE CREDITS

The author tenders his grateful thanks to the following for supplying photographs and illustrations: Di Bailey; Tony Lane; William Lapthorne; Freda Sexton, Goudhurst; Vera and Ron Pope, Littlestone; Trinity House, London; Controller, HMSO, PR Office, Kew; and the British Council. Illustrations and photographs not specifically credited are either by the author or in his collection.

Introduction

The lighthouses of Kent are situated on two types of terrain. North and South Foreland on the high coastal chalkland of eastern Kent overlooking the Goodwin Sands; Dungeness on the extension of the long flat shingle ness of south-east Romney Marsh. As their history and development was also different I have found it necessary to keep them apart the better to tell their story.

However, they all have certain features in common – disasters in the early days of their development; odd inventions intended to improve safety at sea; the first experiments in wireless telegraphy, advances in technology and, ultimately – automation.

Long before the advent of these Kent lighthouses the Romans occupying Kent in the first century AD had built two *pharos* or light towers at Dover. One stood on the Western Heights but now only the foundations remain. The second, built about 46 AD on the opposite side of the valley, can be seen in the Castle precincts, adjoining St Mary Castro church. Anyone standing by its massive octagonal exterior, or within its square ground floor and looking upwards, can judge how impressive it must have been with its eight storeys rising to a height of some 80 feet. The external walls were originally 15ft long at the base and internally 13ft square. The entrance is on the south side, through a 9ft high doorway, and here the base wall is 12ft thick. It is constructed principally of tufa and green sandstone, with layers of bonding courses of Roman red tile bricks set in pink and white Roman cement, which can be seen in the interior. It had wooden plank floors and the holes for the supporting beams are still visible in the perpendicular walls. The storeys were linked by ladders and each had four round-arched windows. At the summit a fire platform was built, probably also on a wood floor but one insulated against the heat by enormously thick stone slabs.

The tower was in a commanding position 380 feet above sea level, and at night the light from its fire, fuelled by coal and wood, would be clearly visible above the local sea fogs to ships voyaging between the Continent and Dover, one of the Roman gateways to England. By day the fire was damped down to create a pall of smoke which also acted as a guide to ships at sea.

Over the years many changes were made to the Dover *pharos*. In the

thirteenth and fourteenth centuries it was altered so it could be used as a belfry. The height was reduced by almost 40ft and the uppermost section of external Roman work overlaid by a casing of flints. Two bells were cast and hung in the tower which was connected to the nave of the Church of St Mary Castro by an enclosed corridor. This connection was severed in 1860 when the church was restored by Gilbert Scott.

Viewed from the pier, shore or town, the Dover pharos, pictured left, is today still an impressive sight. How welcome its light by night and smoke by day must have been to the Roman seafarers at the start of the first millenium.

Alan Major
Canterbury
June 1999

THE NORTH FORELAND
LIGHTHOUSE

Photo: Tony Lane.

1

England's oldest lighthouse

The most north-easterly point of Kent is the North Foreland, the jutting 'nose' of the county, the Foreland being the southern entrance point of the Thames Estuary. Here the notable, almost perpendicular white chalk cliffs in the vicinity, from 60 to 120 feet high, form the front to the sea of the eastern and north-east coasts of Kent, known as the Isle of Thanet. Ptolemy, the Greek geographer, about 150AD, referred to it as the *Cantium* (Kent) *promontorium*, the Romans calling it *Promontorium acantium* and *Promontorium septentrionale*. The monk/historian, the Venerable Bede (673-735) referred to the Isle of Thanet as Tanatos – the name, according to later place name authorities, meaning fire island from the Foreland's blazing light houses. It has been suggested the beacons or light houses were intended, not for aiding seafarers' navigation, but were sited in this area to warn inland Kent of invaders. In the medieval period it was considered a religious duty by monastic and ecclesiastic communities within sight of the sea to warn seafarers, by means of a light, of dangerous sections of the coastline in their vicinity. The Shrine of Our Lady at Broadstairs (Bradstowe) displayed a light in a blue glass lantern and became known to seafarers as the Chapel of the Blue Light. Money was bequeathed to it for the maintenance of the light and in 1451 it was recorded that:

> 'Shippes that lyith in ye narrow sea with marchandyse for Tanet seith at ye hedde of ye cliffe at Bradstowe (Broadstairs) ye Shrine of ye blue light, seith many myle off.'

It is believed that the first beacon was exhibited at North Foreland by 1499, making the lighthouse the oldest established in England. A deed dated that year refers to: 'Ye beecon that lyith at ye hedde of ye cliffe at Beecon Hill'. It consisted of a sturdy 20ft wooden post, at the summit of which was a pivot that formed the fulcrum of a long pole. At one end of the pole was an iron basket containing wood and pitch, at the other end a weight which acted as a counter-balance to the basket. The basket could be raised – or lowered to be refilled – by a chain fastened to each end of the long pole and weighted by a heavy stone. A variation, known as a swape, firelever or lever-light, also in use on dangerous coasts, consisted of a supported upright beam on top of which was a long, tapered pole. From its thinner end, which was directed seaward, hung an iron basket on an iron chain. This basket was kept steady when raised by a chain from its base to the bottom of the upright and the pole was sheathed in metal at its seaward end to prevent it being burnt by the fire in the basket. By swinging the pivoted beam round and downward to the land the basket could be refilled. Another beacon, illuminated by candles, but 'a basket of blazing coals' according to another source, was said to have been sited in the vicinity in 1505.

In 1581 a small tower was built of blocks of local chalk. Mounted on a long pole at its summit was a brazier or iron basket to hold the beacon fire. After the pursuit of the Spanish Armada up the Channel and into the North Sea in 1588 Sir Henry Seymour wrote of sighting it:

> 'Verily my heart filled with thankfulness when ye Rainbow passed ye tower beacon of ye Foreland and we lyith a mile off Meergate (Margate) in ye Isle of Tenet.'

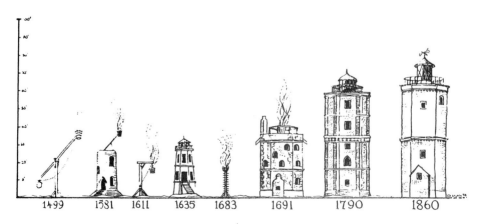

The various methods of illuminating the North Foreland from 1499 to 1860.
Illustration: W H Lapthorne.

9

The exposed chalk blocks were eroded by sea air and frost penetration so the tower had to be replaced, between 1604 and 1611, by a hefty wooden post with a crosspiece from which was suspended a glass lantern containing twenty four candles.

The first true, practical lighthouse was built in 1635/6 by Sir John Meldrum after Charles I, by letters patent in 1635, had granted him a licence to construct and maintain a 'Light House' at North Foreland, with two others at the South Foreland. It consisted of a two storey octagonal tower built of timber, lath and plaster, coated with pitch, illumination being by twenty four candles on a chandelier-like structure and hoisted into position. It proved inefficient, so was replaced by a coal burning iron grate at its summit, although another source claimed an 'oil burner' was used.

According to John Lewis in his *History and Antiquities of the Isle of Tenet in Kent* of 1736, its construction was completed as:

'A House built of timber, Lath and Plaister-work and a coat of pitch to waterproof it, with a large glass Lanthorn on the top of it, in which a Light was kept to direct ships in the Night in their Course, that they might keep clear of the Goodwin Sands which lie off this Point.'

The licence granted to him for fifty years empowered Sir John Meldrum to collect toll dues of one penny per ton from English vessels and two pence per ton from foreign vessels, passing the North and South Forelands, but reduced to a halfpenny per ton if the ship was in ballast. He paid to the Crown £20 per year rent. The North Foreland 'Light House' was destroyed, not surprisingly, by fire. It was burnt to the ground in 1683 and a single, large tallow candle in a glass lantern on a pole was erected as a 'temporary beacon'. It proved ineffective as a warning to seafarers, but eight years passed before a new lighthouse was built.

In 1691 a brick, stone and flint two-storied 40ft high octagonal tower was put up with a coal fire in an iron grate or chauffer, open to the air, to provide the light. In 1698 this lighthouse was recorded as using 100 tons of coal annually. The light stayed 'conspicuous' during calm dark evenings and nights and foggy weather by the keepers using a large pair of bellows to fan the flames of the fire. For their work they received wages of £13 a year, with a rent free cottage and free coal as part of their payment.

A circle of stonework that can still be traced half way up the present lighthouse, was the original summit of the open fire in 1691. It must have been a difficult enough task to maintain the light without receiving the following in a letter, written by the patentee to the North Foreland's and South Foreland's keepers in 1685:

> 'Let ye men at ye lighthouses have a strict charge to be diligent about their fires, for wee hear that ye *Windsor Castle* is lost upon ye South Sand Head; also, pray give all my servants at ye lighthouse a strict charge to be very diligent in keeping good fires this rumbustious weather that no damage may come by their defaults; ask ye Vicar Nicholas White to peep out sometimes before going to bed to see how my lights burn and, if he finds dimness, to reprove ye men. . .'

The licence is believed to have passed through several hands until granted to Robert Osboloston in 1690 to 'hold, erect, change and renew the lighthouses and lights upon the North and South Forelands for 30 years, at the rent of £20 per annum.' When he died his son, also Robert, held the licence for fifteen years, and on his death in 1715 he bequeathed the remainder of the term to the Trustees of Greenwich Hospital which used profits from the light for the maintenance of the hospital and in the caring for seamen patients.

The earliest known view of North Foreland lighthouse, *c*1736.
Illustration: W H Lapthorne.

2

New lights and new lenses

In 1719 the Trustees made an attempt to save money and modernise the North Foreland lighthouse by installing sashlights and enclosing the light in a glass lantern. This was not an improvement. The interior of the lantern became heavily misted with condensation in cold weather or smoke from the coal fire made it difficult to keep the glass clean and clear so seafarers could see the light from a distance. The lantern was removed in 1730 and the original open fire restored.

When the Greenwich Hospital licence expired it was renewed for 99 years and between 1790 and 1793 a further two brick and stone storeys were added to the tower to a design by John Yenn, architect for Trinity House, so increasing its height to 64 feet 7 inches. The coal fire was replaced by oil and in a room described as the 'dome raised on a decagon 12 feet high and 10 feet in diameter,' a patent lamp with reflectors and a magnifying lens was installed. These were 20 inches in diameter.

The dome and the balcony were lined or coated with copper to try to avoid fire accidents. The light was achieved by eighteen Argand oil lamps with concave reflectors 20 inches in diameter (see Dungeness 1792 lighthouse, page 65) and magnifying lenses designed by Thomas Rogers and set into the lantern panes. These were replaced by a new Fresnel type lens in 1860. Lenses designed by William Hutchinson, Dockmaster of Liverpool, were also tried. They were made of hollow glass filled with brine to prevent condensation on the glass freezing in icy weather. Rogers lenses installed in the lantern were of solid glass.

The oil burnt in the early wick lamps used in lighthouses was first of fish, then of vegetable origin. In 1865 a light mineral oil refined from Scottish shale was developed. It had a higher rate of vaporisation and improved illumination. This in turn allowed improvements to the burner by Fresnel, Douglass and Thomas Stevenson who increased the number of wicks to ten. It was, however, Argand's invention in various later forms that was the principal lighthouse illuminant here and elsewhere,

An 1828 engraving of North Foreland lighthouse.
Illustration: Di Bailey

for at least a hundred years and until recently still could be used, as a single or double oil wick lamp, for some reserve systems of lighting.

Some, however, would say that Augustin Fresnel's invention in 1822 of a dioptric or refracting lens was the most important to lighthouse development. It consisted of a framework of lenses – a system of concentric and segmental prismatic bars arranged around a central bulls-eye lens. The prismatic bars were arranged so that rays from a single light source behind the central circular lens would be collected and bent to form and project a parallel beam. Fresnel had taken a number of lens panels and mounted them around an oil wick burner, on a carriage that was made to revolve, and so invented the first flashing lens light with a single light source. He went on to use a stationary cylindrical lens with a shaped central lens and prism segments above and below it so that the light beam was a pillar that could be seen in equal strength all round the horizon. It was this form that was adopted at North Foreland in 1860 to provide an occulting light.

☐ ☐ ☐

3

New owners – and new optics

The Elder Brothers of Trinity House purchased the North and South Foreland lighthouses from Greenwich Hospital in 1832 for £8,336 16s and began to modernise and improve them. They also reduced the dues on British ships to one farthing a ton; to a halfpenny a ton on foreign ships; and made no charge when a ship was in ballast.

In 1920 North Foreland lighthouse was converted to electricity, the optic having 175,000 white candlepower and 44,000 red candlepower from a 3,000w 240v lamp. An acetylene burner was available as a standby in an emergency. It would cut in automatically if the main cable supply and standby generator ceased for some reason. In 1987 this acetylene burner was replaced by a 50 volt 500 watt lamp and new lamp-changer. *The Dover Strait Pilot,* published for yachtsmen and other seafarers, describes the North Foreland light as:

The pre-1987 horizontal lamp-changer.
Photo: Trinity House

'. . . conspicuous from the sea, a light being exhibited at a height of 188 feet (57m3) above Mean High Water level from its 1790 brilliant white octagonal tower situated on the rising ground about 1fi cables within the cliff edge at North Foreland. The tower height, including lantern, is 83 feet, climbed by 106 granite steps, from base to lower lantern, the lantern steps being open ironwork.'

**North Foreland's 240v 3000w electric lamp mounted in the fixed optic lens .
With it is a secondary light for use in the event of failure and an acetylene
emergency light.** *Photo: Trinity House*

The optic is a first order catadioptric fixed lens, the light character being identified by its group flash of five white and red flashes every 20 seconds, occulting every half minute for five seconds. White is visible for 21 nautical miles; red sector 150°-181° for 16 nautical miles, red sector 181°-200° for 15 nautical miles. The red sector glass in the lantern, fitted in 1931, warns shipping of the hazard of shoals over the Tongue Sands off Margate. In 1930 a continuous automatic wireless fog signal with a radius of 50 miles was installed for aircraft as well as shipping. It transmitted on a wavelength of 1,000 metres and used as a signal 'M M F' in Morse It also had a 'radio lighthouse' so inshore vessels with the relevant VHF receiver could get their bearings.

In 1909 Marconi established a wireless experimental station just outside the boundary wall to the north of North Foreland lighthouse. The mast consisted of three steps, and a small shed was transferred to the site from an earlier experimental station at Northdown, Kingsgate. Two masts were later erected on the same site and a wireless station established.

A latticework mast was set up near the site of Marconi's mast and from this wireless fog signal developed the Radio Beacon Service which is still operational at the time of writing. However, it is anticipated that all radio beacons will be discontinued by the year 2000. Eventually a purpose-built coastal radio station was developed in Fairfield, Broadstairs and the operation transferred there from the wireless station near the lighthouse, but the buildings in Fairfield, now boarded up, are still there. The purpose-built station became known as North Foreland Radio.

North Foreland lighthouse, then the oldest working lighthouse in England, was designated as a building of historic interest in 1950. On November 26 1998 North Foreland became the last Trinity House lighthouse to be demanned and converted to being computer controlled and monitored by telemetry from the Trinity House control centre at Harwich.

On an icy windy morning the Duke of Edinburgh, Master of Trinity House, arrived from Manston to perform the demanning ceremony. Accompanied by Principal Keeper Dermot Cronin, he climbed to the

The North Foreland lighthouse complex in the early 1900s.

lantern house to inspect it and to be briefed about the automation engineering. Later he signed the log book, and then went outside to unveil the plaque (pictured on page 7) giving details of the history of the lighthouse. Throughout the ceremony the Trinity House vessels the *Patricia* and the *Mermaid* lay hove to off North Foreland Point in tribute to this historic end of an era.

18

SOUTH FORELAND
LIGHTHOUSE

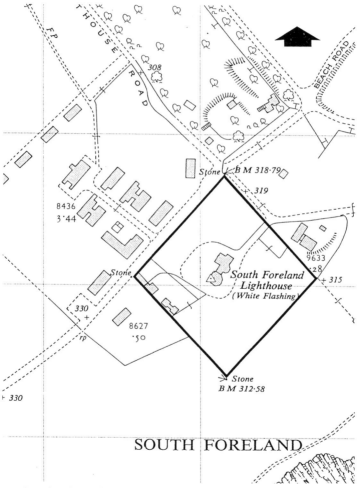

Site plan from the auction catalogue for the sale of the Upper lighthouse in 1989.

1

The first light

The South Foreland is the coastal headland area of south-east Kent between Langdon Bay and St Margaret's Bay. On rising ground, less than a mile south of St Margaret's Bay, stands the South Foreland lighthouse. Here the irregular blocks of chalk faced with layers of flints in horizontal lines that form part of the white cliffs of Dover, made famous in song, rise to a height of 270-300ft. The hazards to passing ships hereabouts is not from vicious currents or reefs and rocks, although the base of the cliffs is fringed with chalk boulders, but from the extensive banks and shoals of sand of the Goodwin Sands, which lie three miles offshore at this point. Between them and the mainland is The Downs, a deep water haven where ships can anchor, but for varied reasons countless vessels and their crews have perished on the 'shippe swallower' – the Goodwins.

The first reference to a light at South Foreland was in 1367 when it was recorded in the accounts of Archbishop Langham that Brother Nicholas de Legh, a hermit living in prayerful seclusion at St Margaret's Strait, had set up a light in a chalk cliff cave to aid passing ships. The Archbishop granted partial indulgences – forty days remission of punishment in purgatory – to those who contributed food and essentials to support the hermit. Medieval monastic and other religious communities within sight of the sea accepted as their Christian duty the provision of lights on the coast to assist seafarers to avoid unseen hazards at night and masses were also said for the souls of those shipwrecked and drowned. It was not enough.

Appalled by their losses in the area shipowners and merchants, petitioned in 1634 for a 'Light House' on South Foreland to indicate the whereabouts of the Sands, but the petition was opposed by the Corporation of Trinity House, which was responsible for providing lights and seamarks whereby the dangers may be avoided and escaped and 'shippes the better come into their portes without peril'.

Trinity House claimed that, in its opinion, a lighthouse here and at North Foreland was unnecessary. The lights would guide in ships of the King's enemies into The Downs; make it easier for wreckers to display false lights; and the light dues would be a financial burden to shipowners and merchants and thus be a grievance to navigation. If a lighthouse was required it would have built one, and anyway its pilots were much safer than a light house.

Despite this claim Charles I granted a Letter Patent in 1635 to Sir John Meldrum, a soldier and a private lighthouse speculator, to erect two white 'Light Houses' with beacon fires, at South Foreland, to warn ships of the Goodwin Sands. The Patent was to exist for fifty years at an annual rent of £20. Sir John also received a Patent to construct the lighthouse at North Foreland, the two lights at South Foreland being also intended to make it easier to avoid confusion with the single example at North Foreland. In 1635/36 Sir John built an Upper, High or Western Light, as it has been variously called, and a Lower or Eastern Light, using timber and plaster. The Upper Light was a considerable distance inland and the Lower Light about 80 feet from the cliff edge.

Sir John was enabled to levy a toll of halfpenny per ton of cargo on passing ships and as soon as Trinity House became aware that there was an annual profit of £1,900 to be made it had second thoughts about a lighthouse at South Foreland. It suggested to the king that it should take over the two 'Light Houses' but received the reply that such a proposal 'comes out of time.'

Meldrum continued to levy the toll, but he must have lost some income as a result of the system by which it was collected by harbourmasters at ports around the English coast where the ships eventually docked. It appears that if the harbourmasters did not receive a sufficient 'contribution' from the lighthouse owner for the sum they had collected, or they fell out for some other reason, they would send his tolls to a rival lighthouse owner in the vicinity. In one instance some of the South Foreland toll money that should have gone to Meldrum was sent to William Bullock at Dungeness lighthouse, who apparently pocketed it.

After two years of such a massive income, Sir John sold a share of his interests in the 'Light Houses', thus spreading some of his liabilities to others. He was killed at the Parliamentary siege of Scarborough in 1645.

The ownership of the 'Light Houses' is uncertain until 1690 when a new Patent was granted to a Robert Osboloston or Osbolton on a thirty year term. In 1705 Osboloston's son, also Robert, took over for seventeen years. He did not live at the lighthouse or in the vicinity of St Margaret's, instead hiring two men at £13 a year plus accommodation and fuel – a low wage, which they had to supplement by fishing during the day. The two lights burned thirty two chaldrons of coal annually, at a cost of around £1 10s per chaldron or small cart load. Osboloston also had the two men spied upon. He asked the vicar, William Barney, and a Mr Chitty, the parish assessor for rates, to inform him if the two men neglected their duty of maintaining a bright light. For this service each spy received a chaldron of coal from Osboloston but perhaps their heart was not in the task for they let the two men go unreported and Sir John Byng, sailing by in 1707, complained to the Admiralty that he could 'scarcely see the light all night long'.

Osboloston, Junior, died in 1715. He bequeathed the lighthouses and land to the Trustees of Greenwich hospital who were soon expressing their concern at the cost of maintaining the two fires at South Foreland. They were advised, by Trinity House of all people, that by controlling the combustion about two thirds of the fuel cost could be saved, so the open fires were enclosed in glass lanterns. For the same reason, in 1730, here and at North Foreland, the lanterns were taken down and the 'Light Houses' returned to their original design with open coal fires, tended by men on a part-time basis – fishing usually, perhaps smuggling too, being their other 'employment' .

In 1729 George II had authorised the Trustees to increase the toll on passing ships 'having benefit of the said lighthouses to one penny a ton, the cost to be shared between the ship's master/owner and owner of the cargo, when divided.

□ □ □

2

New lamps for old

The introduction of parabolic reflectors to concentrate and throw forward horizontally the light rays from lamps placed in their foci was a big improvement in lighthouse illumination. At about this time – the late eighteenth century – the revolving frame carrying the lamps and reflectors was also introduced. This mode of lighting is called the catoptric or reflecting system as opposed to the dioptric or refracting system where the illumination is created by a central lamp, the rays from the latter being transmitted through a combination of lenses which surrounds it.

In 1793/4 the Trustees of the Greenwich Hospital decided to rebuild the Upper lighthouse, which they did at a cost of £1,804 2s 3d. It was three storeys high and had a copper lantern to enclose the light now provided by Argand lamps burning sperm oil, on the catoptric (reflecting) system and found that the clusters of small lamps, each one with a metallic reflector behind it, made it easier to keep the glass clean.

In 1795 the Lower lighthouse was built. It was similar to the Upper but two rather than three storeys high and also with Argand lamps burning sperm oil in conjunction with the same catoptric system. In 1810, magnifying lenses were installed and when, around 1845, sperm whale oil became scarce and costly, it was replaced by colza or vegetable oil although this did not give the same quality of light.

Robert Stevenson, lighthouse engineer, after a visit to the South Foreland, referred in his *Survey of Lighthouses, Beacons and Lights* of 1813 to the 'apparatus' as 'fitted up· in the modern style' with twelve to fourteen plated reflectors in each lightroom which were not thoroughly cleaned and some reflectors 'in a rather dirty state'. He also noted that: 'The dwelling houses partake of that cleanliness which is so general in the cottages of the English.' At this time the annual profit from the toll was some £1,000.

The Upper lighthouse was entirely altered in 1843 and rebuilt to the

The bullseye of the lens at South Foreland lighthouse.
Photo: Trinity House.

design of James Walker, Chief Engineer to Trinity House, which had acquired the South Foreland lighthouses from Greenwich Hospital in 1832. The tower of the new lighthouse had a square exterior with a castellated parapet and a four-wick burner with dioptric apparatus for diffusing the light was installed. Cottages for the keepers were built beside the stone tower. In 1846 the Lower lighthouse, 385 yards distant, was also rebuilt as an octagonal stone structure 49 feet high, to a design of James Walker. The cost of improvements to these lighthouses, with the new dioptric lens and lamps, was £4,409 4s 3d

The light quality was further improved in 1852 when a dioptric fixed white light was installed, enhanced by a reflecting lens, nineteen zones of prisms and two spherical parabolic reflectors. Michael Faraday,

Scientific Adviser to Trinity House, persuaded that organisation to investigate converting South Foreland lighthouses to electricity and several lighting experiments were held.

By 1853 Professor F H Holmes had developed a 'new magneto-electric apparatus' to generate electricity for lighthouses. Experiments with it had powered the Dubesq carbon arc-lamps in tests in the Trinity House Blackwall depot and South Foreland was chosen for preliminary trials. In 1857 the 'apparatus' was established in an engine house near the Upper Light and on 8 December, 1858, when two of Holmes' magneto-electric generators were tried the strongest artificial light then known was produced. Driven by a steam engine rotating at 85 revolutions a minute the generators had achieved a brilliant light visible from the gallery of a lighthouse on the French coast twenty seven miles distant. However, it was thought doubtful that the blue-white light of the arc would penetrate fog as efficiently as the yellow light produced by oil lamps.

The Lower Light carried on displaying a light from the standard oil lamp and reflectors so that ships could compare the two systems in identical conditions. As the arc light carbons were consumed they had to be adjusted by hand, but even though the light produced was the strongest artificial light known and superior to that of oil lamps, it was found difficult to control and rather erratic. South Foreland had, however, become the first lighthouse in England to be lit by electricity, even if only for a short period from 1858 to 1859.

Another experiment at about this time, was an unsuccessful trial of limelight as an illuminant in lighthouses. Limelight, devised by a Lieutenant Thomas Drummond, was produced by combustion of oxygen and hydrogen on a surface of lime. Oil continued to be used until January, 1872, when it was abandoned at South Foreland after the electricity system was finally approved by Trinity House and Holmes' improved magneto-electric alternating current machines running in parallel at 600rpm was installed there. These machines supplied electric power to the lighthouse for some fifty years and South Foreland can be considered to be the first lighthouse in England in which electricity was permanently installed.

In 1872 Chance Brothers of Birmingham arranged both the Upper and

Lower light towers 'in their optical portions'. James Chance designed the optics which comprised a third order dioptric fixed apparatus built so the light from the refracting centre was directed on the sea in graduations from the horizon up to two-thirds of a mile from the tower.

In 1876 experiments had been undertaken with the German Siemens dynamo-electric system and it proved superior to the 'apparatus' of Holmes but this remained at South Foreland to power it until 1922. At this time South Foreland's staff consisted of one electrical engineer and six keepers, paid three shillings and ninepence a day. A Major George Elliot visited them and later reported the keepers to be:

> '. . . very intelligent men who seemed thoroughly to understand the magneto-electric machines and who gave me an accurate account of their operation. One was by trade a watchmaker, another a stonemason.'

Three of the four temporary lighthouses used for fuel tests, with the Upper light-house in the background. *Photo: Trinity House.*

3

A testing time

The successor to Faraday, Professor John Tyndale, for several years after 1874 also carried out experiments on fuels for lighting. In 1869 land between the two lighthouses was purchased for the erection of engine houses, workshops, and living quarters for staff. For test purposes a row of four temporary wooden lighthouses, painted white and with large letters A, B, C, D on their sides, was put up in alignment with the two permanent lighthouses. The gas and electricity required for the fuel tests had to be produced on site, but among the various other fuels tried mineral oil was found to be the most cost effective at that time, although oil and gas lights suffered by atmospheric absorption. Electricity, despite its tendency to loss in bad conditions, overall produced the strongest intensity. Tyndale's report on experiments stated:

> '. . . that for ordinary necessities of lighthouse illumination mineral oil is the most suitable economical illuminant and that for salient headlands, important landfalls and places where a very powerful light is required electricity offers the greatest advantage.'

Tyndale also used South Foreland as one of the lighthouses for other types of tests, one being on the relative merits of sound-producing instruments for fog signalling and how the propagation of sound was affected by different climatic conditions. Various types of sirens and whistles were imported from North America for testing at South Foreland but were found to be inefficient in the prevailing weather conditions of the locality. He found a signal gun was more efficient than gongs and bells, and the firing of a 24 lb howitzer was even better.

The temporary experimental lighthouses were also used by Sir James Douglas to test proposed improvements in the ventilation of lighthouse lanterns. Another electrical 'first' for South Foreland was in 1922. The development of high power electric filament lamps and the availability of mains electricity supplies meant the end of the hard-to-control arc lamps and the Upper Lighthouse was the first in Britain to be equipped with a 4 kilowatt electric filament lamp and be connected to and lit by mains electricity.

Trinity House had decided to obtain electric current from another source in 1919, but it was not until March 1922 that it was obtained from the Dover Electric Supply Company's mains which were extended the several miles to the lighthouse and St Margaret's. When the mains supply was switched on the old Holmes magneto-electric apparatus was switched off. Even so, an emergency generator and large accumulators were kept in the basement in case of any disruption in the electric supply.

4

Wireless links ships to shore

Guglielmo Marconi, the Italian pioneer of wireless telegraphy, was to provide yet another 'first' in the history of the South Foreland lighthouse. With the permission of Trinity House he installed his Wireless Telegraph and Signal Company's (later the Marconi Wireless Telegraph Company) equipment in a small room in the engine house and used it with the East Goodwin lightship in his experiments into wireless telegraphy as an aid to navigation and a means of telegraphic communication between ships and the shore.

On 24 December, 1898, he established an over-the-sea communication between the lighthouse and East Goodwin lightship anchored 12 miles away on the east side of the Goodwin Sands. This was the first occasion wireless was used in a British lighthouse. The apparatus had been conveyed to the lightship in an open boat, set up in a single afternoon, and was immediately ready for use. The experiment was deemed to be successful and communication by wireless between lighthouse and lightship came into regular operation.

After watching this experiment and examining the apparatus a scientist, Dr JA Fleming, wrote in wonder to *The Times:*

> 'Marconi has placed a lightship on the Goodwin Sands in instant communication day and night with the South Foreland lighthouse. A touch of a key aboard the lightship suffices to ring an electric bell in a room at South Foreland lighthouse 12 miles away, with the same ease and certainty with which one can summon the servant to one's hotel room. An attendant now sleeps hard by the instrument at South Foreland.
>
> If at any moment he is awakened by the electric bell rung from the lightship he is able to ring up in turn Ramsgate lifeboat and, if need be, direct it to the spot where its services are required within a few seconds of the call for help. In the presence of the enormous practical importance of this feat alone and of the certainty with which communication can now be established between ship and

shore without costly cable or wire, the scientific criticisms which have been launched by other inventors against Signor Marconi's methods have failed altogether in their appreciation of the practical significance of the results he has brought about.'

According to the records of the Marconi Company the first use of wireless telegraphy as an aid to ships in distress occurred on 11 March 1899 when the sailing ship *Elbe* ran on to the Sands. East Goodwin light-ship communicated with South Foreland lighthouse by wireless and soon local lifeboats were standing by but the *Elbe* refloated on the next tide. The second occasion was on 28 April 1899 and this time it was the lightship itself which was involved. The SS *R F Matthews*, outward bound, collided with it and inflicted severe damage. The lightship telegraphed South Foreland lighthouse which informed Trinity House, Ramsgate but lifeboat assistance was not needed.

Even while the East Goodwin lightship and South Foreland lighthouse experiments were taking place Marconi had in mind a more ambitious role for wireless telegraphy at South Foreland. The Marconi Company had sought permission from the French Government in September 1898 to construct a wireless station on the French side of the Channel but the request did not receive official approval until 2 March 1899. When it arrived the company carried out a survey of the Boulogne area and decided on a site at Wimereux three miles north of Boulogne. The wireless station was built by the 26 March that year and was ready to attempt to communicate with South Foreland lighthouse 28 miles away. At Wimereux the following day Marconi met a commission of army, navy and telegraph service representatives appointed by the French Government. A special correspondent was present from The *Times.*

Marconi himself was at the transmitting key to send the first international wireless message between France and Britain – across the Channel from the station's mast at Wimereux to the lighthouse. The witnessing authorities set test messages for onward transmission to varied prominent people in England, these being successfully received and forwarded to their respective recipients by overland telegraph. The witnesses for the French Government were impressed.

On 28 March the South Foreland lighthouse also received the first international wireless press message when *The Times* correspondent reported 'communication between England and the Continent was set up yesterday morning by the Marconi system of wireless telegraphy.' *The Times* correspondent reporting the event also achieved the first inaccuracy in an international wireless press message when he stated the distance between South Foreland and Wimereux was thirty two miles when it was actually twenty eight miles.

It would appear that the successful establishment of contact by wireless telegraphy over this distance meant its commercial potential was assured. There was a snag. When there was communication between two stations it was satisfactory, but if another wireless station within range began to transmit the radiations spread out over a number of frequencies, and the transmissions jammed each other,

To solve the problem one idea was to ration the transmission time of every station. Each would have the exclusive use of the system for a stated period and then would have to cease transmitting to allow others to do so. The second and more practical proposal was to try to reduce the spread of the radiation. To this end a number of experiments were set up with the three stations at East Goodwin, South Foreland and Wimereux involved in the tests. Within a short time there had been sufficient progress in reducing the spread of radiation to enable South Foreland to communicate with East Goodwin without a single dot being received by Wimereux.

Following this success more demonstrations were arranged before representatives of the French Government which had placed the warship *Ibis*, also the storeship *Vienne*, at the disposal of the Marconi company. The *Vienne*, with Marconi on board, steamed in the English Channel and a series of test communications were made with South Foreland on 17 June, 1899, which proved to all present that there had been a great improvement in station selectivity.

Dr J A Fleming wrote again to *The Times*:

'During the last few days I have been permitted to make a close examination of the apparatus and methods employed by Signor Marconi in his remarkable telegraphic experiments between South Foreland and Boulogne and at the South Foreland lighthouse have been allowed by the inventor to make experiments and transmit messages from the station there established, both to France and to the lightship on the Goodwin Sands, which is equipped for sending and receiving either wave signals. Throughout the period of my visit, messages, signals, congratulations and jokes were freely exchanged between the operators sitting on either side of the Channel and automatically printed down in telegraphic code signals on the ordinary paper slip at the rate of 12 or 18 words a minute. Not once was there the slightest difficulty or delay in obtaining an instant reply to the signal sent.'

Even so, despite these successes, the use of wireless appears to have lost favour with Trinity House, which did not retain the system and instead had submarine cables extended to the East Goodwin and other lightships from the shore. In the First World War, for security reasons, the use of cable was temporarily discontinued. Eventually, in March 1923, due to the development in wireless telephony with valve transmission and reception, Trinity House returned to wireless and installed a Marconi telephone on the North Goodwin lightship for experimental trials with Ramsgate Post Office. The trials were entirely successful and the apparatus easily operated by members of the lightship crew, so submarine cables were abandoned and wireless telephones fitted.

The Marconi Company used the South Foreland lighthouse again for an experimental transmission, in September, 1925. This was of a radio guidance system in which an aerial 'like the three wings of a triplane', according to a newspaper report, revolved every two minutes sending coded signals. Marconi's yacht, *Elettra*, cruised the Goodwins area for seven hours and British Government and shipping officials on board watched the system give all the ships within a hundred miles an index letter that would indicate the *Elettra's* position – information that could prove to be vital in poor visibility.

South Foreland Lighthouse.

5

Changes of use

The 1903 Admiralty *List of Lights* described the South Foreland as having two fixed electric bright lights shining from white towers, 69 feet and 49 feet in height set in line North 85 West, 385 yards apart. They formed a leading light seen clearly from the south end of the Goodwin Sands. In 1904 a revolving, more powerful lens was removed from St Catherine's lighthouse, Isle of Wight, and installed in the Upper lighthouse at South Foreland. It was turned by an ingenious clockwork mechanism by which the keeper could wind a small weight up a shaft in the centre of the tower. The rotating lantern weighed more than a ton but it stood on a bath of mercury and there was virtually no friction to the heavy optic. As the weight descended it set off a warning bell so the keeper knew it was time to start winding again.

Also in 1904 the Lower lighthouse was closed by the Trinity House as a seamark and dismantled – for two possible reasons. The one commonly held was that it was because there was a risk of the cliff collapsing into the sea. The second, and more likely reason, was that as a result of the southerly drift of the Goodwin Sands, the transit line of the Upper and Lower lighthouse towers no longer indicated a safe passage – the Upper Light being misleading. It was modified and upgraded and deemed sufficient, without any repositioning and reinstatement of the Lower Light.

The latter reverted to the Ecclesiastical Commissioners who sold it with the keeper/engineer accommodation and surrounding land to a London solicitor who converted lighthouse into a luxurious home. A condition of the sale was that no light was to be lit in the lantern, which the new owner used as a sun lounge, unless curtains were used to screen it.

Between the wars the Lower Light was used as guest accommodation by the occupier of the adjacent house. It was requisitioned by the Ministry of Defence in 1939 and after the

The Lower Lighthouse in 1986.

34

war, as a result of its occupation by the army, it was in too bad a state to be lived in. However, it remained as a spectacular centrepiece of the garden that surrounded it and in 1967 it provided the eerie setting for the 1967 Warner Brothers film, *The Shuttered Room,* starring Oliver Reed and Flora Robson. Bricks from the towers of Professor Tyndale's temporary light-houses were used to pave a path to the converted Lower Light, which is now being used as a store. It is on private land and inaccessible to the public.

In the Second World War South Foreland lighthouse was under the control of the Admiralty but manned by Trinity House personnel. It was only used, displaying a light at half-power, if an Allied convoy was pass-ing through the Dover Straits. An exception was on 12 February 1942 when the German warships *Scharnhorst, Gneisenau* and *Prinz Eugen,* heavily escorted, made their successful dash in bad weather through the Dover Straits. The vessels were first spotted from a naval lookout post sited at the bottom of the lighthouse garden and South Foreland dis-played a light to act as a beacon to guide any British aircraft returning from attacking the German ships. There were none.

In 1943 the lighthouses of South Foreland, North Foreland and Dungeness housed secret transmitters to jam German radar installations on the French coast. It was also in 1943 that the lantern and lens of the Upper light was smashed when hit by a shell from German long range guns on the coast of France.

At the end of the Second World War normal service was resumed at South Foreland for several years before the lantern room was fitted with electric motors to drive the optics and the light operated by remote con-trol. As a result of this automation only one keeper or caretaker was required and it became a 'man and wife' station.

Trinity House finally declared South Foreland lighthouse redundant and closed it on 30 September, 1988. Later it was put up for sale by ten-der and was described in the sale catalogue as an 'early Victorian light-house with attached accommodation. Tower section adjoining to cottage, connected by a corridor'. When it was in use the visible range of its one million candlepower intensity light was 26 miles in clear weather and its characteristic was 'white group flashing three times every 20 seconds'.

The height of the light above Mean High Water was 374 feet and the lighthouse had five floors reached by a spiral staircase of 65 steps. There was no fog signal.

It was bought by the National Trust the following year and is now a listed building maintained by that organisation. A keeper's cottage that had been demolished when the lighthouse was automated, has been rebuilt by the Trust to restore the configuration and symmetry of the complex of buildings which used to be interconnected but are now three separate entities.

South Foreland Upper Lighthouse is in first class condition with its original equipment, including the turntable weighing two tons that revolved the light. It is open to the public from Easter to October on Saturdays, Sundays, Bank Holiday Mondays 2pm-5.30pm. There is an admission charge and access, on foot only, is from National Trust car park at Langdon Cliffs or from St Margaret's-at-Cliffe village, at end of Lighthouse Road.

THE GOODWIN LIGHTSHIPS

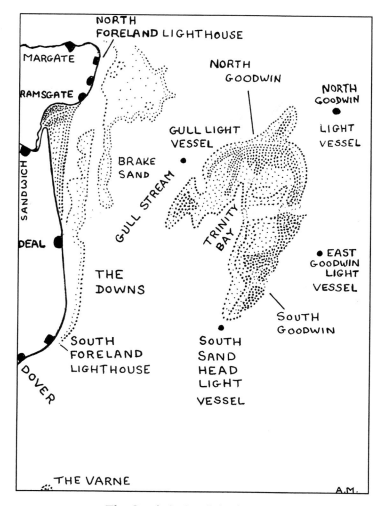

The Goodwin Sands in the 1920s

1

Ye Shippe Swallower

A very dangerous flat – and fatal,
Where the carcases of many a tall ship lie buried.
The Merchant of Venice. Act 3, Scene 1

The infamous Goodwin Sands are situated some four miles east of Deal on their western side and six and a half miles or so on their seaward side. At their longest they stretch for more than ten miles in a north-east to south-southwest direction from North Sand Head to South Sand Head. At their widest they are four and a half miles across. The sandbanks and channels of the Goodwins continually alter shape and position, almost as if alive when on the move. In the 1930s more sand was exposed at their north end, but more recently a greater expanse has appeared at the south end. The greatest quantity of sand is exposed by the late summer tides. The Kellett Gut has a history of vanishing and reappearing and the area called South Calliper near South Sand Head, so named because of the shape of the exposed sand, disappeared in the 1970s.

When exposed, areas of the Sands can be walked on in comparative safety, although at the fringes, even in the calmest of weather, there is turbulence in the sand and adjoining water. Quicksand is also an ever-present hazard. There are also small channels or water passages, known as 'swashways' or 'swatchways', that are only navigable in small boats by experienced men who know them and their changing, restless habit.

In spite of these dangers people picnic on the Sands; cricket and golf matches are played there; and a popular pastime is treasure hunting with metal detectors. At high water the Sands are submerged and revert to being the 'ye shippe swallower'.

In 1974 a plan was put forward to build a third London Airport on the Goodwin Sands, with a huge harbour and a giant tanker complex. This, like so many vessels that have come to grief on the sands, vanished and was never heard of again. I wonder why?

In 1800, in the tenth volume of his *History and Topographical Survey of the County of Kent,*1800, Edward Hasted wrote of the Goodwins:

'This sand consists of a more soft fluid, porous, spongious and yet withal tenacious matter than the neighbouring sands and consequently is of a more voracious and ingurgitating property so that should a ship of the largest size strike on it in a few days it would be wholly swallowed up by these quicksands that no part of it would be left to be seen and this is what makes the striking on to it so much more dreadfully dangerous than on any of the neighbouring ones which are of much more hard and solid nature.

'When the water is off these sands become exceeding hard and firm insomuch that many people land and stay hours on them for pleasure in summer but when the tide becomes to cover them they become soft and so float to and fro with the waves and when they retire settle the same as before. The redness they occasion in the water is plainly discerned from Deal and its neighbouring shore'.

The Goodwin Sands are basically in two parts, the North Goodwin and the South Goodwin, divided by the Kellett Gut. On the south-west edge is Trinity Bay and west of it is the wide channel known as The Downs. On the north-west side of North Goodwin, from opposite Ramsgate to almost opposite Deal, is the Gull Stream. The North Goodwin is somewhat semi-circular and the North Goodwin lightship was formerly moored at its east-north end. The South Goodwin, which had the South Sand Head lightship at its south-west end, has been likened to a lobster's leg and claw. Although they are dangerous the Goodwin Sands do serve as a breakwater and create between them and the coast a natural deep water anchorage, The Downs, some eight miles long and several miles wide, varying in depth from 4 to 12 fathoms.

Apparently the Sands were used as a means of defence in the early to mid-seventeenth century and possibly earlier. An account in *Naval Tracts* published in the reign of Charles I, states:

'A ship riding at The Downs and fearing a surprise attack from an enemy in the night, with a southerly wind, by placing two boats with lights on either side of the Brake will direct one how to pass the Channel and around the Sands which being done and the lights taken away, the ship that pursues them will run upon their death if they follow.'

As early as the seventeenth century a petition was raised to anchor a ship burning candles as a light to warn off other ships. The Brethren of Trinity House ridiculed the proposal, asking how a ship could be kept on this anchorage using only hemp ropes (chain mooring not being available until 1880). The candles, they said, would be ineffective and are there men willing to crew it? Ship owners did not agree with them. Robert Hamblin and David Avery, realising a fixed lighthouse was not feasible, established the first lightship in English waters at the Nore Sand, at the entrance to the Thames, in 1732. It was so successful that a second was positioned off the Dudgeon Shoal, twenty five miles southeast of Spurn Head in the centre of The Wash approach, in 1736.

These first lightships were conversions of wooden hulled merchant ships such as small Dutch hoys, and the light would consist of four to six candles in a lantern hoisted to the masthead – or in thecase of the Nore lightship, suspended from each end of a yard on the single mast. Sails were at the ready in case the vessel broke adrift. The problems of anchoring in poor holding ground were overcome by using bridle chains of immense strength with weighty 'mushroom' anchors, so called because of their shape.

It was at about this time that Henry Taylor, master mariner, devised a plan to put a 'floating light' on the Goodwins. When offering his plan to Trinity House, he said that in his seafaring career there were no signal lanterns to guide vessels into ports and some of the lighthouse lights were so bad he had known ships to anchor and fire guns to wake up the sleeping lighthouse men to stir up their fires. And he added:

> 'We know one person who, while he lay in The Downs, saw thirty ships lost on the Goodwins . . . through mistaking one Foreland light for another – a case that often happens and is often attended with fatal consequences but which the floating light will effectively prevent'.

Taylor also wanted a lease of the light, perhaps to obtain some toll money as recompense, but he got neither light nor lease. Years later, when he had retired ashore and was in straitened circumstances, friends put pressure on Trinity House and in 1796 it begrudgingly admitted Taylor's plan was of use and made him a grant of £500.

2

Lightships go on station

The success of the Nore lightship as a navigational aid also meant that Trinity House had to reconsider its objections to lightships. A wooden hulled ship was purchased, converted to a lightship and placed at North Sand Head – the North Goodwin position – in 1795. It was replaced eventually by an 184 ton three-masted iron vessel specially built at Blackwall at a cost of £5,587. This had a fixed light on each mast and its hull was painted bright red with the name in white letters. In 1877 the light was changed to one flashing white light 36 feet above the water, giving three quick flashes per minute and visible up to ten miles. There was also a gong for striking in fog.

It was decided, after fourteen years on the trial, that this lightship had been a success. In 1809 a 158 ton wooden lightship was positioned in the Gull Stream on the western edge of the Goodwin Sands. It cost £4,197 and had *Gull* written in large white letters on its side. Two fixed lights shone from a yard on its single mast. This ship also had a fog gong. In 1825 the ship was given two masts, each with two lights, and in 1860 the characteristic was altered to one flashing white light, with a flash every twenty seconds visible for ten miles. In 1856 the *Gull* lightship was run into by an American vessel and the lantern lamps extinguished but in three hours repairs had been made and the lamps relit. In March 1929, after long service, the vessel then on station was withdrawn for an over-haul and another lightship, No. 38, was towed out to the Gull station and the crew of the withdrawn lightship transferred to her.

Her career on this station was brief. During the night of 18 March 1929, at 4am in thick fog, the Ellerman liner *City of York* struck No 38 on the port side near the master's cabin and cut her down to below the waterline amidships. The *City of York* anchored and sounded an SOS on her siren. The damage to the lightship was so extensive that she sank quickly into 7.5 fathoms of water. Her crew were rescued with the exception of the master, Captain Williams who was trapped in his cabin and

The Brake lightship on station after her refit in the 1930s.

drowned. Next morning only the daymark of No. 38 was visible. Divers entered the vessel and recovered the master's body then examined the ship. It was considered worthwhile to attempt to salvage her, and this was done successfully with lifting gear in July, 1929. The vessel was beached at Deal for temporary repairs and then towed to Ramsgate to be made seaworthy.

A local vessel stood on the lightship's station temporarily, then a light buoy was positioned there. After repairs and a refit on the Tyne, No. 38 was returned to the Goodwins in 1930. However, as a result of changes in marking of the narrowing navigable Gull Stream channel, caused by alterations in the Sands, she was positioned on the western side, some four miles from Ramsgate and three and a half miles from Deal, closer to the Brake Sand, which was shifting in a south-west direction. The station name was changed from *Gull* to the *Brake* lightship and, after 120 years, the continuous marking of the Gull Stream had come to an end.

Even though closer to the coast, life could still be hazardous for the crews of the *Brake* lightship. It, along with other lightships, was also sometimes used as a place of refuge for shipwrecked crews. In thick fog on 22 November, 1935, the Norwegian steamer *Tres*, two miles to the south-southeast, collided with and sank the steamer *Lancresse* of Guernsey. The *Tres*, although with badly damaged bows, hove to by the *Brake* lightship and transferred the ten surviving members of the eleven man crew of the *Lancresse* to the lightship. Ramsgate lifeboat was called up by radio to take the rescued men ashore.

On 16 January, 1940, several vessels were anchored in The Downs when one of them, the Italian steamer, *Ernani*, dragged her anchor and drifted on to the *Brake* lightship striking it with force on the bow to near the waterline and then drifted away. The crew abandoned the lightship and eventually reached the safety of the guardship HMS *Holdfast*. The lightship, however, stayed afloat, so the crew reboarded her, patched up the damage and the vessel was towed stern first to Harwich to be repaired and then taken to the Mouse station. In 1941 she was withdrawn and towed to Great Yarmouth where she was laid up for the duration of the war after which Thurrock Yacht Club bought her, in June 1947, to use as a boathouse. When, after the war, most lightships were returned to their previous stations, the *Brake* lightship was not repositioned. She was replaced by a light buoy.

In 1832 a third lightship was ordered, this time for the extreme southern end of the Goodwin Sands, about four miles east-northeast of Dover, opposite St Margaret's Bay. The 184 ton single-masted wooden vessel was specially built at Blackwall at a cost of £3,212. It had one light giving two white flashes every half-minute visible for ten miles; the hull was painted red with *South Sand Head* in white letters; and in 1875 a foghorn was added. In 1885 this lightship was struck by an unknown vessel, one side of her hull was stove in and her lantern destroyed.

On 28 December 1899, the *South Sand Head* lightship's moorings parted and she drifted to the edge of the Goodwin Sands and because of the ferocity of the gale it was not possible to rescue the crew until three days later. When the winds died down a Trinity House tender towed the undamaged lightship back to her station and the crew reboarded her. In 1904 another collision damaged the lantern of the *South Sand Head* lightship and in December, 1914, she broke from her moorings again and drifted. On 24 March, 1929, the German steamer, *Oliva*, collided with the

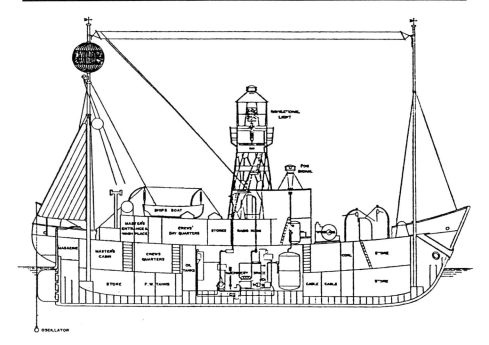

Sectional plan of a 90 class lightship.
Illustration: British Council 1947

lightship which fortunately remained afloat and was able to be towed to Ramsgate for repairs. It was returned to station on 18 April.

After the Second World War the No. 90 lightship – a modern vessel, 104 feet long, built by Philip and Son of Dartmouth, in 1937 – was allocated to the South Sand Head station as the *South Goodwin* lightship. The vessel was to make world news headlines on 28 November, 1954, when she broke her moorings and was driven by one of the most violent gales in living memory up the western side of the South Goodwin Sands and struck them almost opposite the *East Goodwin* lightship, whose crew could only watch helplessly as the *South Goodwin* lightship capsized and all seven crewmen were drowned. The only survivor of the catastrophe was a civilian working aboard the vessel, which was a total loss.

An old lightship, No 65, was put into position as a replacement until

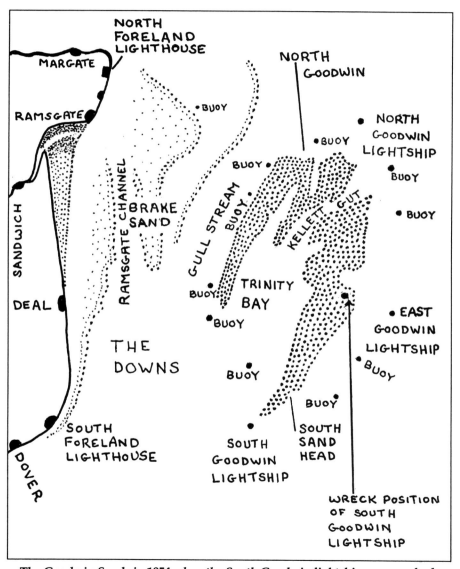

The Goodwin Sands in 1954 when the South Goodwin lightship was wrecked.

January, 1955, when a new lightship, No 17, was put on the station for many years.

In 1874 a 163 ton wooden vessel, with a fog gong, known as the *East Goodwin* lightship, had been sited one and a half miles east of the 'Back of the Sands', as the outer or eastern edge was called. It had one light, seen every fifteen seconds, and visible for ten miles. This light was green to warn ships to keep to the east while sailing past. The lightship carried the standard equipment of two signal guns, rockets and other pyrotechnic devices so should a ship be seen to be sailing into danger the guns were fired or if a ship did run on to the Sands rockets could be set off to tell the coastguards immediate assistance of a lifeboat or steam tug was required.

On 1 December, 1903, the *East Goodwin* lightship was struck by the 722 ton ship *Hazelmere* and, after temporary patching, was towed into dock for numerous leaks to be repaired. On 12 November, 1961, the *East Goodwin* lightship dragged her moorings and was driven southwards on to the edge of the Goodwins by a north-east gale, then away from them towards the *South Goodwin* lightship. She managed to stop using a temporary anchor and after three days, when the gale abated, the still afloat vessel was towed to safety.

In the section on South Foreland the involvement of the *East Goodwin* lightship in early experiments in ship to shore wireless communication is fully described. Trinity House had given permission for the experiments and in December, 1898, these had reached the stage for a demonstration of the system's practicality. Once established it worked well for more than two years and was involved in successfully saving several vessels and numerous lives. The lightship itself benefited on two occasions. Once when part of its bulwarks were carried away in a violent gale and secondly when a ship collided with it. Immediate assistance was forthcoming on both occasions, through messages sent to South Foreland lighthouse. In an Admiralty court case proof was established that £52,588 worth of property had been saved as a result of one brief wireless message reporting a steamer had run aground on the Sands. Thus early in the history of wireless it had been proved of vital value to shipping, to safeguard property and lives.

Details published for seafarers of the last Goodwin lightships are:

South Goodwin is a red light vessel with name in white letters on the hull sides, the light being exhibited at an elevation of 40 feet above the waterline, moored one and three quarter miles south-southwestward of South Sand Head. Has a fog signal.

North Goodwin is a red light vessel with name in white letters on the hull sides, the light being exhibited at an elevation of 40 feet above the waterline, moored about one and a half miles north-eastward of North Sand Head. Has a fog signal,

East Goodwin is a red light vessel with name in white letters on hull sides, the light being exhibited at an elevation of 40 feet above the waterline, moored about one mile eastward of the

To reach the lantern of the *South Goodwin* lightship it was necessary to climb the rigging – not an easy job in a gale.
Photo: Kent County Journal

Goodwin Sands. Has a fog signal and transmitting radio beacon, the aerial spanned between the two masts.

In the vicinity there was also the *Tongue* lightship off Margate, and the *Varne* lightship off Folkestone.

□   □   □

3

Life on the lightships

The modern lightships were two masted with the light in a lantern mounted amidships on a steel lattice tower support, its optic being an assembly of specially designed mirrors and with filament electric lamps adjusted to the type of flash required. The fog signal and horn were sited above the deckhouse clear of any obstructions that might blanket the sound. The ships were linked to the shore by wireless telephone and each had a crew of seven – the master, two lamplighters, two fog signal drivers and two seamen who were rated and received extra pay when maintaining and operating navigational aids. Steps on the promotion ladder started at seaman, the next stage being fog signal driver then lamplighter and finally, after some fifteen to twenty years service, master. The seamen served one month afloat followed by a fortnight ashore. The master was relieved every month and did turn and turn about with another master ashore. The master had a cabin aft and in it was the wireless telephone which, with the ship's log and papers, was his responsibility. Members of the crew were either on or below the main deck, the accommodation being divided to provide a radio beacon room, machinery space, a magazine, oil and water tanks, stores and cable lockers. The lifeboats were on the upper deck.

Christmas aboard a lightship was not so bad, according to William High-Lawson, a one-time member of the crew of the *South Goodwin* lightship, writing in *Kent Life* in December 1963:

> '. . . the oracle is usually worked so that one person cooks for all hands and the Watch list is slightly bent so that the one who will do the cooking is the one who is best qualified for the job . . .'

He also recalls the arrival of 'the stalwart band of friends who would annually visit the lightships of Kent, invariably bringing a great deal of Christmas fare'. The mayor and his party from Ramsgate, laden with turkeys, puddings and other festive treats, were always taken out to 'their' lightship, the *North Goodwin,* a week before Christmas usually, but not always, in the local lifeboat. Now the lightships have been automated these visits have ceased.

In the Second World War some of the lightships were intermittently manned, their lamp only being lit to aid a passing convoy. They were sitting ducks for the Luftwaffe pilots who attacked, damaged and destroyed the vessels that were there for the of benefit of friend and foe alike. The *South Folkestone Gate* lightship was attacked and sunk and two of its crew members killed.

Some lightships, among them the South Goodwin, were fitted with Decca Navigator instruments incorporating an alarm which sounded if the ship moved off station. These alarms were so sensitive that they would sound if a large amount of cable was paid out. Early lightships had fixed lights. Later revolving apparatus was introduced with oil wick burners focused in silvered copper reflectors and flashing characteristics introduced. The 8ft diameter lantern was centralized around the single mast and supported by a chain so that it could be lowered by day for cleaning and trimming the wicks, and hoisted aloft at night to exhibit the light. Later lanterns were fixed at their correct height and electrically lighted, as were the navigational light and general lighting of the ship and crew quarters, with diesel electric generators providing the power. The compressors that charged the fog signals air reservoirs were driven by two sets of diesels.

During the day the lightships displayed a distinctive daymark at one or both mastheads. When off station these daymarks were lowered, and at night all lights were extinguished except for a red light at the stern and bow. Lightships were also known as 'dumb vessels' because they had no means of propulsion and had to be towed to and from their moorings. In open water the lightship rode at a single anchor, usually mushroom or, before these were made, an anchor with a stock to give a good holding in bad weather. When positioned in a channel or in tidal waters the lightship rode to a mooring with two anchors, which acted as 'flood' and 'ebb legs'. The anchor cables were attached to the bows by a swivel piece which would allow the vessel to swing around it and remain on her correct station.

Provision had to be made for the rolling and pitching of the lightship in order to keep the light beams horizontal. This was effected by mounting the optical apparatus with its illuminant on a pendulum-balanced table, the whole assembly being in gimbals to allow it to swing. The swing of the pendulum was adjustable and when set up the apparatus was arranged to have an oscillation just out of step with the natural period of the ship's motion.

A pendulum-balanced multi-catoptric apparatus had a two-tier optic made up of four sets of superimposed mirrors mounted in pin hinged frames. At the top and bottom of the frames were quadrant plates that could be set to any pre-arranged position and by manipulation any characteristic from one to four flashes could be produced. Some lightships had dioptric apparatus of a special multiphase design that was similarly mounted but the optic was made sectional and symmetrical about its horizontal axis so that by rearranging the panels, and inverting of some of them, any characteristic from one to four flashes could be shown.

Economics and technical developments eventually meant the end of the three manned lightships. They were replaced on station by Automated Light Vessels (ALVs). The first to go was the *North Goodwin* lightship on 10 August, 1985, but the ALV on the North Goodwin station was itself subsequently withdrawn on 22 April, 1988, being replaced by a High Focal Plane Buoy, still there at the time of writing, marked NE Goodwin. The second was the *East Goodwin* lightship on 22 August, 1985; the third the *South Goodwin* lightship on 31 October, 1985, both the latter two stations at present still having Automated Light Vessels. The vessels were monitored from North Foreland lighthouse until 1995 when the task was transferred to Trinity House, Harwich.

The *Varne* lightship was replaced in 1987 by a Large Automatic Navigation Buoy (LANBY) fitted with a light and fog signal, but it was later withdrawn and replaced on the Varne station by an ALV.

4

Other plans to light the Sands

As well as lightships other methods, some weird and wonderful, were attempted to warn vessels that they were nearing the dreaded Sands. One of the first was to scuttle an old ship with its mast, topped by a ball, visible above high water. The mast was secured by chains to the stem and stern of the vessel which was sited on the east South Goodwin Sand near to Trinity Bay. It was soon wrecked and washed away.

In 1841 Deptford civil engineer William Bush, came up with the idea of a light-tower beacon. A large cast iron caisson was to be made at a Yorkshire ironworks; transported by sea in sections to Deal to be assembled in the naval yard there; and towed to the chosen site and sunk to a level bed at a depth of about 64 feet. The sand inside it would then be removed and replaced by rocks and granite, and to this 120 ton foundation would be bolted a cast iron structure, 86 feet high, having on top of it a 40 foot housing for a lantern and gallery.

All did not go well with the caisson of Mr Bush's light-tower beacon. The vessel towing it to the Sands on 22 October 1841 ran aground and so the caisson had to be cast adrift in rough weather. It was rescued by another ship and taken back to Deal where it sank. It was salvaged, taken to pieces, re-built and in July, 1842, was towed back to the Sands and on to the North Calliper. There it was allowed to settle to the bottom and by 12 September had reached a depth of 25 feet. It continued to sink but on 15 October it was overturned when a ship collided with it.

Two years later Bush salvaged the caisson and rebuilt it only to have it damaged by a gale down to low water mark. In 1845 the caisson was again salvaged and resunk and work started on a revised plan for the superstructure, lantern and gallery. It was almost completed by July 1845 when Trinity House informed Bush that his light beacon was in a totally unsuitable situation in the middle of the Sands and vessels would be lured to disaster by its light. It was, in fact, the Admiralty that had chosen this site for the beacon not Bush, but he had to dismantle it. With it went his scheme for a continuous seawall, formed by a series of coffer-dams, to enclose the Goodwin Sands so they would become a haven or harbour of refuge for distressed seafarers.

Similarly, in 'a humble but earnest effort to save the lives of ship-wrecked mariners of all nations' Captain (later Admiral) Frederick Bul-lock RN, with the co-operation of the Admiralty, devised a 'Refuge Beacon' which took the form of a 40 foot high timber mast or shaft, 13 inches in diameter, bearing a trelliswork gallery which would hold 'twenty people in comfort or thirty crowded together'. A blue flag could be displayed from a light flagstaff as a signal when aid was required.

The mast was sunk in the sand through a strong oak frame in the shape of a cross secured by four iron bars weighted with ballast, and supported by eight chain shrouds or stays in pairs attached to iron piles 17ft long driven into the sand. The gallery, which was stocked with food, water and spirits, was positioned 16 feet above high water mark. To reach this refuge it was necessary to climb up the central shaft by means

A drawing by S Owen, 'taken of the spot', of Captain Bullock's first safety beacon.

of the iron steps fixed to it or make use of the rope ladder. Exhausted seafarers unable to make the climb could be hoisted up with blocks and ropes in the large basket chair that Bullock had thoughtfully provided for the purpose.

On 10 September 1840 the 'Refuge' was floated out to the Sands and, with the help of the crew of HMS *Boxer*, it was successfully erected and Lieutenant G Boyes, RN 'ascended to the gallery amid much cheering'. It survived for four years, until 6 August 1844 when it was run down and damaged by the carelessness of a passing Dutch galliot. The 'Refuge' was replaced during 1844, with 50 to 60 ton blocks of rock, chalk and shingle as weighting, and stood for a further three years until it disappeared in a gale in October, 1847.

These misfortunes and mishaps did not deter others from investing money, time, energy and effort into schemes to make the Sands safer for seafarers. A Mr Steward, a civil engineer, attempted to erect a single pile beacon on the eastern edge of the Goodwin Sands in 1843, finally completing it in September 1844, only for it to capsize. He tried again on a different site with a similar lack of success.

On 6 July 1844 James Walker erected a beacon which survived until 1850 when it was taken down by Trinity House as it had been moved by the shifting sands 450 feet to the west where it could be a hazard to vessels. He built another in 1847 but that vanished. In 1849 Trinity House erected the last beacon on the Sands and amazingly it remained in place for thirty years, until destroyed in a storm.

It should be said that some of these schemes were not undertaken in a casual hit or miss manner. The reasoning behind Captain Bullock's tower refuge beacon was sensible for often seafarers escaped from their stranded ship onto the exposed sand only to be drowned when the tide covered it. And the captain took the precaution of employing experienced engineers to find out for him at what depth there was a firm foundation for the structure.

Attempts were also made to determine the composition of the Sands. Boring augers were used and at a depth of 7ft 6ins different sands, seashells, stones, and flints were found in some sites while in others the sand was dense and the suction strong enough to bend the augers and make boring there impractical. In yet other sites at a depth of 15 feet the sand changed to blue clay and then hard chalk.

Another survey was carried out in October 1849 by Sir J A Pelly, the Deputy Master of Trinity House. Iron shafts, 10ft long and 2ft 6ins in diameter, were sunk and the contents pumped out. The shafts sank into sand until at a depth of 78ft, they reached a bed of hard chalk. The depth of water inside the Goodwin Sands to the bottom was 9 to 10 fathoms while the depth outside the Goodwins, where the outer edge is sheer and steep, is 15 fathoms.

A WRECK ON THE GOODWINS.

The Goodwin Sands were, and still are, a hazard to ships passing through the Dover Straits. They can swallow a stranded vessel in less than an hour, or it can stay evident for generations, or disappear and reappear at intervals . . .
Illustration: Di Bailey.

□   □   □

THE DUNGENESS LIGHTS

The 1690 fire tower of Dungeness.
Illustration: W H Lapthorne.

1

The early lights

The most southerly part of Kent is Dungeness (pronounced Dunjieness) at the seaward extremity of a large, triangular expanse of shingle extending into the English Channel. It is to the southeast of the three marshes that form the area known as Romney Marsh and is approximately four miles southeast of Lydd, Kent's southernmost town. The ness, which covers several thousand acres, is an apposition beach – an accumulation of shingle, shingle-sand and saltmarsh. Sand, deposited over a considerable period of time, has been shaped and added to by wave action from two opposing currents, one running approximately south south west and the other east north east. It continues to extend by between eighteen to twenty feet a year and at its highest it is some twenty feet above sea level.

In the Kentish dialect of Old English the word ness was used for a point, cape, promontory or foreland. In the West Saxon dialect of Old English the word was *naess* for these terrain examples. In Old English *nesu*, *nasu* and *nosu* were all words for nose, closely related to *naess*. John Leland, an English antiquary who journeyed throughout the country between 1535 and 1543, said of the area in his *Itinerary in England:*

> 'In the midway betwixt Romney town and Lyd the marsh land beginneth to nesse and arme (project like a bent arm) in to the sea and continueth a pretty way beyond Lyd and running into a poynt it standeth as an arme, a foreland or a nesse.'

William Camden, in his *Britannia – Kent*, published in 1586, said much the same:

> ' . . . the land runs out a great way east, which we call ness, q.d. nose. . . On the extremity of the point which we call Dengenesse is nothing but gravel and pebbles.'

In *A Perambulation of Kent*, published ten years earlier, William Lambarde described it as a neshe, adding, 'before this neshe lieth a flat into the sea, threatening great danger to unadvised sailers'.

Numerous ships were wrecked on the ness or in the vicinity, with immense loss of life and cargoes. The hazard was supposedly compounded by Lydd church, 'the cathedral of the marsh'. Seafarers claimed that in certain light conditions the 132 feet high tower of the church, viewed from the sea across the flat landscape and against the sky, took on the appearance of 'the forme of the saile of some tall shippe', lulling them into a false sense of safety.

In an attempt to prevent the losses of ships, crews and cargoes John Allen, a goldsmith of Rye, applied in 1612 for permission to erect a 'light house' at Dungeness. The income from it appears to have been intended for the coffers of Rye Corporation.

Allen lacked influence and, even more importantly, financial support so did not obtain the necessary patent. But in August 1615, Sir Edward Howard, Cupbearer to King James I and Admiral of the Narrow Seas did. The patent granted to him and his heirs for fifty years, in spite of objections from Trinity House which had an alternative proposals for the ness, gave him authority to levy a one penny per ton toll on ships that sailed past the 'light house' he planned to build about a hundred yards from the sea.

The wooden tower he constructed had, at the summit, a platform with an open brazier fire, almost certainly with an iron base and frame to hold the burning coals. Bags of coal were hauled up the outside of the structure by block and tackle.

As a financial speculation it was not a great success. Sir Edward found it a difficult and frustratingly lengthy process collecting the tolls due to him as the ship owners and ship masters did all they could to dodge paying the debt. Eventually he sold his patent to another member of the royal household, the Clerk of the King's Kitchen, William Lamplough, who prudently obtained the assistance of the Crown, via its Customs Officers, to collect the tolls due from the ships' masters at the ports where they docked.

Although they admitted the light at Dungeness was advantageous to the safety of their ships sailing in this part of the Channel the ship owners – now unable to avoid payment of the tolls – claimed it was a 'nuisance to navigation'. They allied themselves with Trinity House to have a Bill promoted in Parliament whereby the patent for the light could be withdrawn from Lamplough. The attempt failed – Parliament choosing not to interfere with the King's grant of a patent. In 1623 Lamplough reduced the tolls to a halfpenny a ton following complaints about the efficiency of the light. Later, in an attempt to 'keep a better light', he changed from burning coal and wood to using candles but although they gave a more constant light their power and range was small even when lit in groups.

The area of the ness was continuing to expand and in 1635 Lamplough demolished the tower built in 1615 and replaced it with one sited closer to the sea. It was 110 foot high, had living quarters at the base and a light fuelled by coal which was hauled up the exterior of the tower in a basket. The wood engraving on a toll receipt issued on December 10, 1703, by the Customs Office at Portsmouth to Choise Claison, master of *The Bunch of Grapes,* shows the coal hauling operation in progress. The keeper can be seen tending the blazing fire in a huge fire basket at the summit and opposite him, from an iron jib and pulley, hangs a basket full of coal.

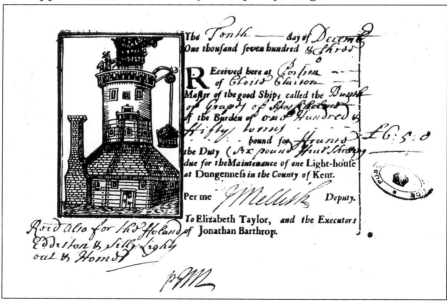

The toll receipt with its wood engraving.

Around the base of the tower is a single-storey structure with a tiled roof, an outside brick chimney, and windows and a door – presumably the keeper's living accommodation.

It must have been a hard task to maintain a bright, steady light throughout the hours of darkness on this site, especially in winter or during stormy weather. The light might be clearly visible on the leeward side in a gale, but hard to see, if at all, on the windward side. If wet and windy any illumination from the flames would be partly or completely hidden by smoke.

When a new lighthouse was built at St Agnes in the Scilly Isles in 1680 an attempt was made to protect the fire and overcome the problem of smoke. Above the cast iron grate containing the coal fire was a glass lantern with ventilation funnels. Unfortunately, while this offered some protection, the glass in the lantern was quickly blackened by the sooty smoke and had continually to be cleaned by the keepers.

Sometimes there were difficulties in getting regular supplies of sufficient coal to the site for the fire, which on a night of strong winds, would consume several tons. The fuel had to be brought to the ness by sailing collier, then offloaded on to hoys or barges and dumped on the shore, from where it would be manhauled to the lighthouse. This was the method used at Spurn Head on the Humber for on record are complaints from keepers there about the difficulty of hauling carts of coal over the shingle and sand to their light house. Alternatively, the coal could have been taken by collier to Rye and then carted laboriously to the light house.

Some of the owners of the privately owned lighthouses had difficulty obtaining the toll money owed to them and, as a result, the keepers were poorly, frequently irregularly, paid. This encouraged a certain amount of bribery and corruption for the keepers were in a position to be of use to others. Some had their palms greased by agents employed by unfriendly countries and on occasions the Dungeness light keepers were bribed in this way. They warned French and other ships – almost certainly those with contraband aboard – when British naval ships were in the sea area or in local harbours. They did so by a pre-arranged warning signal – simply tipping buckets of ashes over one side or the other of the tower to indicate the direction the smugglers should avoid.

Perhaps even those employed to apprehend the offenders were paid to look the other way for on the night of January 13 and 14, 1736, a large quantity of tea was landed at Dungeness and the Commissioner of Customs, on getting wind of this, thought the Customs House Riding Officers and Waterguard officers might have been somewhat lax.

An examination was made of the logbooks of these men to ascertain where they were at the time. The inquiry showed they were all on duty where they should have been and the Waterguard's revenue cutter was actually cruising in Rye Bay on the night of January 13 and had then anchored at Dungeness Point during the night of the fourteenth. No one had seen a thing, neither smugglers nor tea.

Lamplough lost the patent in 1655 – during the Commonwealth when Oliver Cromwell was Lord Protector. Why is unknown but probably because his political views and allegiances were not the right ones. From 1647 to 1660 a Commission took control of all lighthouses, including those of Trinity House, the controllers of which were believed to have royalist sympathies.

Members of the Commission did not find the task of providing and maintaining the light easy, so they appointed a patentee of their own choosing to do the same tasks as Lamplough. He got into arrears with the rent due on the site leased for the light. and the land owner, the Earl of Thanet, warned that he would have the 'light and house' pulled down if the rent was not quickly paid up to date.

The patentee appealed for the Commonwealth Parliament's protection against this threat and it was granted because Parliament considered it was not satisfactory that 'the safety of many lives and the State's should be left to the will of the Earl of Thanet'. It is not certain what this 'protection' was – possibly it was just time to pay – but in the meantime the land owner was not allowed to put his threat into effect.

After the restoration of Charles II in 1660 there was confusion about who should hold the patent of the Dungeness light. Lamplough, according to the Commonwealth, had, due to his adherence to the Crown and royalist sympathies, forfeited his right to it. The Commonwealth-appointed patentee refused to leave the light claiming he held title by purchase from the Commonwealth. It must have been resolved somehow because in 1690 Richard Tufton, Earl of Thanet, who lived at Hothfield, was given 'the grant of the light' by Charles II. After his death it came into the possession of his son-in-law Thomas Coke of Holkham, Norfolk, the lightkeepers at the time being John Harden and John Lane, supervised by Charles Coxsell of Lydd. It appears that there was no gender discrimination about who could be a patentee for later in the seventeenth century the patent for collecting the tolls passed to one Elizabeth Shipman.

By 1746 the coal fire light was again a considerable distance from the sea due to the growth of the ness. Trinity House claimed it was misleading, as did the ship owners, who also repeated their earlier complaint about the poor quality of the light, but surprisingly, nothing much was done. In 1776 Thomas Coke's nephew, also Thomas Coke, became the owner of the 'light house' at Dungeness and the site situation continued to worsen until 1790 when Trinity House demanded that a new lighthouse be built.

Thomas Coke agreed to demolish the 1635 lighthouse, the location of which is marked today by some old coastguard cottages, and to construct a new one nearer the sea.

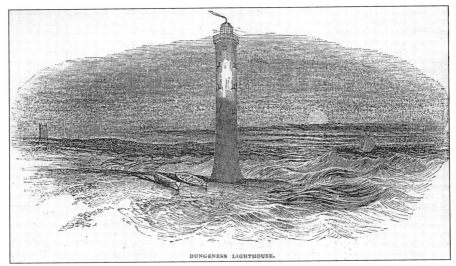

DUNGENESS LIGHTHOUSE.

An artist's impression of the 1792 lighthouse, published in the *Illustrated London News* in 1843, gives some credence to the claim that the tower of Lydd church, on the left, could be mistaken for a sailing ship.

2

The 1792 lighthouse

Samuel Wyatt, consultant engineer to Trinity House from 1776 to 1807, was commissioned by Coke to design and build a new lighthouse nearer the sea in 1792. The final cost was £3,159 0s 4d. The tower stood 116 feet high and was similar to the classic design of John Smeaton for the third Eddystone lighthouse.

The foundations were on shingle and could, unless they were widely based, have caused problems. Hague and Christie suggest in their *Lighthouses – Their Architecture, History and Archeology,* that Wyatt overcame these difficulties by following the Eddystone design and using the construction method Smeaton employed for his Spurn Head brick tower lighthouse. Weight had to be kept to a minimum. To achieve this Wyatt first drove in four concentric rings of three metre long wood piles within a 10.35m diameter circle. Approximately 102 abutting sheet piles are thought to have formed the continuous circle of the outer ring and the inner rings had about 108 piles. Both inner and outer rings were capped with a wood sleeper beam. Carefully positioned stone, radially set, was rammed into the intervening area. The intention was to bind the foundations so that any settlement would be evenly distributed. Brick footings were 2.15 metres but narrowed to 1.25m at the cellar stage and to 0.61m at first floor, the remainder of the structure being 48 metres thick. The fuel store or cellar and the floor of the coal-fired lantern both had a brick vault, the intermediate floors being of wood.

One problem was encountered during its construction. The 116 feet high tower had seven storeys with a wooden connecting staircase. The original design had a stone staircase which began so close to the outer wall that when it had reached twelve feet it was realised by the builders that the conical shape of the boundary wall would stop it being taken any higher. Three years after the lighthouse's construction a second problem occurred. The first storey developed cracks and sturdy buttresses had to be built to strengthen the entire structure.

According to one source the 1792 lighthouse was financed by a grant from George III to Margaret Tufton Coke, Baroness Clifford and Countess of Leicester. Every British and foreign ship contributed towards its support, dues again now being at the rate of a penny per ton.

The following account of the lighthouse appeared in the *Illustrated London News* on February 11, 1843:

'The Dungeness lighthouse is a fixed light, of Argand lamps, with parabolic reflectors, the method by which the majority of the coast of Great Britain is lighted.

'The Dungeness establishment is not an expensive one, the great item of expense being the oil, which, in one year, costs £220 and £300 for salaries and allowances, but the Commission for collecting the dues exceeds £700. An agent at Lydd provides the oil, etc., and attends to repairs, for which he receives £40 a year and there is but one light keeper, whose solitariness reminds one of the cure for misanthropy: "Go and keep a lighthouse for a fortnight". Men of average intellect can scarcely be found to become lighthouse keepers'.

Because of the design of the tall lighthouse tower – wide at its base to

**The 1792 round house and East and West cottages, all used as keepers'
accommodation, pictured in the 1960s from the top of the 1904 lighthouse.**
Photo: Freda Saxton

spread its weight and counter dangers of settlement – there was ample
space for living accommodation for the keepers (rather giving the lie to
the *Illustrated London News* account of one solitary keeper). The accommodation took the form of a surrounding 'round house' painted black to
match the bottom section of the lighthouse's exterior with its two broad
black bands, one at the top, one at the bottom, and a broad white band in
the middle.

The wall of bricks and posts which formerly acted as a boundary
around the base of the 1792 lighthouse and the round house has long
since been removed. In the nineteenth century two cottages were built
close by, also as accommodation for the keeping staff. The round house
was sold by sealed tender at auction in 1993/4, with the adjoining cottages, and has been converted into private accommodation.

The exact position of the new lighthouse is recorded in Bagshaw's
Gazetteer for Kent of 1847:

'A lighthouse was erected at Dungeness Point, 4¼ miles south southeast from the church (Lydd) in 1792, on the plan of the Eddystone Lighthouse. It stands about 500 yards south of the old (1635) light house and is 100 yards from the sea at high water.'

It was illuminated not by using coal but by oil, seventeen Argand oil burners being mounted on a frame supported by ten pillars, each lamp having a concave reflector twenty inches in diameter. The oil was sperm (whale) oil and later vegetable oil was used.

The early oil lamps used in some lighthouses had problems with smoke which discoloured the glass unless the wicks received regular attention. The Argand oil lamp burner used at Dungeness had been invented ten years earlier by Aimé Argand. It had a circular wick with a central draught of air and a glass chimney so the steady flame was brilliant – and smokeless. Its concave reflector, which directed a beam of intense light, may have been of glass but this would have been extremely heavy. It is

more likely to have been of a lighter material such as the handbeaten silver and copper which was used with the Argand oil burners elsewhere by 1800. With later modifications this burner was to be the chief method of illumination used in lighthouses for the next hundred years. It was only replaced as recently as 1901 by the Kitson vaporised oil burner.

Dungeness lighthouse was struck by lightning on Christmas Day, 1821 and the oil-filled lantern caught fire. Tragically one of the lighthouse keepers looked upwards to note the damage and was blinded when lead from the roof, melted by the heat, dropped on to his face and splashed into his eyes. According to one source the other damage was minor, the masonry on the north side being cracked. This crack was filled in with cement and

Detail from an 1823 aquatint by William Daniell of the lightning strike. *Source: W H Lapthorne.*

then painted over. Another version of the incident states that during a severe thunderstorm the lighthouse was struck by lightning, the tower being damaged from summit to base. Repairs costing about £1,000 had to be made and three copper bands, like hoops around a barrel, were used to strengthen the tower. A new roof was needed and the lighthouse repainted red and white so it would be more conspicuous in daytime, or so it was thought. The lighthouse supervisor in 1821 was Stephen Terry of Lydd.

On August 27, 1818, Robert Stevenson, who was responsible as Engineer for fifteen important lighthouses, inspected Dungeness. In his report he says:

> 'Find the tower had been in danger of falling and was secured by four buttresses. The light is 16 feet in diameter and has 18 reflectors which were made 16 years since by Mr Howard of Old Street. I would set reflectors differently and have not more of them than at present.'

The reference to Mr Howard indicates that the reflectors had been obtained in 1802 from him whereas the other Trinity House lighthouses at that time had the same reflectors, but they were supplied by Howard's rival, George Robinson.

3

The coastal blockade
and the Low Lights

Smuggling was rife along the entire stretch of the coastline from Gravesend marshes eastwards but principally from Sheerness to the Isle of Wight. In 1816 Captain William 'Flogging Joey' McCullock of HMS *Ganymede*, a frigate used between the North Foreland and Dungeness in the campaign against smuggling, was given permission by the Admiralty to test his coastal blockade plan. It involved the navy putting armed crews ashore after dusk along the coast to patrol during the hours of darkness and returning them to their ships before dawn broke.

A trial between the North and South Foreland was deemed a success and in 1818 the second phase of the Royal Naval Coast Blockade for the Prevention of Smuggling was set up on a permanent basis. It covered three areas – North Foreland to the Isle of Sheppey, North Foreland to South Foreland and South Foreland to Beachy Head. These areas were divided into sections, the Dungeness section stretching from Romney to Camber. It had a series of guard houses on the coast and use was made of the barracks and Martello towers that had been built when Napoleon threatened to invade England.

Smuggling was reduced and eventually declined into insignificance, but it is open to question whether this was due to the Coast Blockade and its replacement, the Coast Guard which was set up in 1831, or to the tax reductions which made avoiding payment of duty no longer economic.

Captain McCullock did not live to see the end of smuggling. He died at the Port Admiral's residence in Deal in 1825, aged 45, and was buried in St Leonard's churchyard, Upper Deal, where there is a wall tablet to what some would say is his infamous memory.

In September, 1817, a Royal Navy ship had sailed past Dungeness and the ship's captain was astounded to discover the lighthouse was not emitting a light. He reported this to Trinity House, which demanded an explanation from the lighthouse supervisor, Benjamin Cobb who replied to the effect that the nineteen year old keeper had been ill that day and unable to climb the tower to light the light and his assistant was too unreliable to do the task. The assistant was dismissed and Cobb was 'retired'. The owners had to apologise.

In 1826 the Trinity House Board, noting that members of the Coke family had received a lucrative income from the Dungeness light for a considerable number of years and their lease was going to run out in 1828, urged the Lords of the Treasury not to renew it. A Select Committee had, four years previously, recommended uniformity of tolls with the same charge for each light and that Trinity House should buy out all the private lighthouses, including the one at Dungeness. Their Lordships agreed with the Trinity House proposal, then changed their minds and granted the Coke family a twenty one year lease, at a yearly rental of £20, on condition tolls were reduced to a halfpenny and a portion of surplus dues were divided equally with the Crown.

The Cokes still received, in four years of the renewed lease, an average of £3,218 annually. In 1832, for example, the toll produced £2,066 for the Crown and the same amount for the Cokes. However in 1836 this private enterprise came to an end. An Act of Parliament enabled Trinity House to purchase Dungeness from Thomas William Coke for £20,954, the lease still having twelve years and 175 days remaining.

In 1861 the 'magneto-electric apparatus' developed by Professor Holmes and tested at South Foreland was installed at Dungeness. The *Kentish Express* said of it:

> 'Dungeness. The Electric Light has been started here permanently since the 6th of June and is the same magnetic light which was first tried at South Foreland on 8th December, 1858, and from August 1859 to March 1860, with perfect success. It was placed at Dungeness in October 1861, although not started till June, 1862. It shows the most wonderful light that has yet been exhibited in a lighthouse.'

It was used at Dungeness for thirteen years until 1875 but, as at South Foreland, it turned out to be expensive and unreliable because of voltage fluctuations. Cored carbons were tried in the powerful arc lamps but the flame of the arcs was difficult to control and gave an irregular light.

Electric power was replaced in 1875 by a large oil lamp of 850 candle-power surrounded by glass prisms which increased the intensity so its light was visible for sixteen miles.

The shingle had continued extending into the English Channel, increasing the distance between the lighthouse and the sea, so Trinity House decided, in 1880 and again in 1909, to try and improve the situation by erecting smaller subsidiary lights and foghorns nearer to the sea. In addition to the light from the tower, which was useless in thick fog, other means had been used to warn ships of the ness and their proximity to it. One method was to use rockets, two being fired every five minutes. However, if the fog remained dense for a long time a considerable number of rockets had to be used.

An alternative was a fog bell which was suspended from the tower and rung by hand. The one at Dungeness was removed when the lighthouse was transferred from private ownership to Trinity House but later a very big bell, hung on a wooden stand, was sited near the lighthouse and rung loudly during fog. It was replaced about 1860 by a fog trumpet operated by compressed air and powered by a steam engine. To vary the notes of the foghorn to whatever was required by the weather conditions – loud, shrill or deep – tongues of iron of different thicknesses were inserted.

The first oil powered revolving low light, or half-light as it was sometimes called, was about forty feet high. It was built in 1880 beneath a semi-circular corrugated iron sheet roof and had a two wick burner which consumed two gallons of oil per night and gave out a white light equal to eighty candlepower, with a bright flash every five seconds, visible for ten miles. The foghorn sounded a high note followed by a low note in quick succession every two minutes. It was powered by a device known as Ericson's Caloric Engine and was nicknamed the Cow and Calf as the sound it made was supposedly like a cow answering the call of her calf. Previously this foghorn was operated by compressed air produced by a coal fired engine which consumed considerable amounts of fuel and needed constant attention to keep it working in foggy weather.

An experiment was carried out at Dungeness to operate the foghorn with an oil fired engine. The machine tested was Priestman's Oil Engine which had been awarded the Royal Agricultural Society Silver Medals at

The Low Light of 1880, to the left of the then operative Trinity House experimental station, pictured in 1929. *Photo: Vera and Ron Pope.*

The 1904 Low Light as it appeared in 1945. *Photo: Margaret Barnes.*

Nottingham in 1888 and at Windsor in 1889. The *Kentish Express* reporter who covered the tests in the 1890s thought highly of it.

'This engine, suitable for any driving purposes, requires no coal, no boiler, no furnace, no driver, is quickly started, requires little space and works any-where,' he wrote. 'It has certainly stood its tests well during dense fogs. If any-thing it discharges a bigger blast of sound than the old one. This engine, which works admirably, will in all probability be adopted at every lighthouse station on the coast'.

The second low light or half light was built in 1904, replacing the by then obsolete 1880 example. It had a revolving, white flashing light, and a fog siren that gave three blasts – short, long, short – at two minute inter-vals. It was oil powered, consuming two gallons overnight, and produc-ing an 11,000 candlepower beam visible from a distance of seven miles.

In 1937 one of the local children, Vera Oiller, then aged 13, made a detailed record in an exercise book of *Our Village of Dungeness,* and in it gives these precise details:

'The light in the foghorn is a white revolving light and the fog signal is a dia-phone. The flashes of the fog horn are one and three tenths of a second and the eclipse is three and seven tenths of a second. The sounding is short, long, short. The short blast lasts for one and three quarter seconds and then there is silence for two seconds, the long blast is three seconds then there is another silence for two seconds; then a short blast again and between the two sets of blasts there is 107fi seconds of silence, the total amount of time with the blasts and the silence is two minutes'.

A Romney, Hythe and Dymchurch Light Railway engine, hauling crowded carriages, steams past the 1904 lighthouse.

4

A railway and a new lighthouse

In 1873 the Rye and Dungeness Railway and Pier Company was incorporated to develop the potential of Dungeness as a train ferry terminal. However, nothing came of the company's grand plans for a railway or pier, but the rights to go ahead with the scheme passed to the South Eastern Railway in 1875.

On December 7, 1881, the nominally independent Lydd Railway Company – which was taken over by the South Eastern Railway in 1895 – opened a railway line from Appledore to Dungeness, but only for the carriage of goods, passenger trains terminating at Lydd. Later the line was upgraded to carry passengers to Dungeness.

The South Eastern Railway was also actively interested in Dungeness and purchased land in the area for £5 an acre. It had all sorts of schemes in mind including plans for a railway from Appledore to Headcorn via Loose, then to Maidstone, where it would link up with the line to London. If this had come about boat trains could have been run from London to Dungeness for a Dungeness to Boulogne Channel crossing in competition with the Folkestone route.

Lydd Railway Company was granted authorisation by an 1882 Act of Parliament to construct a branch line from Lydd to New Romney. The three mile stretch was completed in June, 1884, and its terminus was called New Romney and Littlestone-on-Sea, the last named being the sea-side resort that was expected to spring up to cater for the huge influx of visitors the new line would bring to the area. But like harbour and pier at Dungeness Littlestone-on-Sea did not materialise. Rail traffic on the new line was low and not until the area was opened up by new roads did the holiday camps come along and the seaside homes proliferate.

The railway line at Dungeness terminated within a few yards of the lighthouse. The station was a small weatherboarded building with a curved corrugated iron roof. Alongside it, also on the short, single plat-form, was a shed. All that remains today are the remnants of the plat-form and some posts. The railway track has been removed and the site is fast returning to nature.

In the meantime the South Eastern Railway had capitalised on its investment in the acres of shingle by excavating and transporting it out by the truckload.

'Dungeness of late years has opened up considerably,' reported the *Kentish Express*. 'This is chiefly owing to the South Eastern Railway extending their line to within a hundred yards of the lighthouse, which is, of course, a great boon to those in the neighbourhood. The traffic could not possibly pay the S.E.R. Company but they possess what may be called, to them, a small gold mine. Having purchased many acres of this beach (at £5 an acre) they are carrying it away in large quantities. It affords a splendid material for them in repairing their own lines, while they sell it to other companies and also for the purposes of public and private residences.'

The only present day reminder of this commercial activity are some old gravel workings. In a sad way they are memorials of what might have happened if the harbour and pier had been built. Would the region have become of large economic importance, with a busy rail system and industry attracted to the area by its proximity of France? Or would it, if built and developed, have failed to compete successfully with nearby Folkestone and Dover?

In 1929 the Romney, Hythe and Dymchurch Railway extended its line from New Romney and opened a station at Dungeness, mainly for holidaymakers to visit the ness and the lighthouse. This caused the now Southern Railway to realign the New Romney branch line, which it did in 1937, creating two new halts, Lydd-on-Sea and Greatstone-on-Sea, again mainly for holidaymakers. When the realigned line opened the line to Dungeness was closed to passenger traffic but remained open for the carriage of goods until 1953. In March, 1967 the New Romney section

This aerial view of the 1904 lighthouse shows the Romney, Hythe and Dymchurch line with its station and restaurant and, nearer to the tower, the Southern Railway spur to the Dungeness lighthouse terminal. *Photo: Margaret Barnes*

also closed and now all that remains is the track from Appledore to near the Dungeness nuclear power station for nuclear waste to be transported out of the area.

The continual extension of the shingle ness meant a new lighthouse was inevitably required. In 1901 work began on the fourth lighthouse, originally known as the High Lighthouse. It was built by Pattrick and Company of London fifty yards from the base of the 1792 tower and first lit on March 31, 1904. It is now called the 'old' lighthouse, in comparison with the 'new' 1961 lighthouse.

The tower is 143 feet high and it is said that three million bricks were used in its construction. The light was a pressurised paraffin lamp of 164,000 candlepower. This consisted of an incandescent mantle into which paraffin oil was vaporised by compressed air at a pressure of 60lbs to the square inch. The ignition rod in the centre was heated for twelve minutes by methylated spirits before the lamp was lit, the light being located centrally in line with the lenses in their facets. Each facet of the light casing had a surround of prisms to concentrate it on the lens in the centre.

The light burned two pints one gill of paraffin per hour – the smaller light below the main light one pint per hour. There was storage space on the ground floor for about eight hundred gallons of paraffin. This was pumped up, as required, to a twenty-five gallon tank in the lantern room. The light was lit at dusk and burned continually until dawn. The lamp was, of course, not extinguished between its visible flashes. It burned continuously but the reflectors around it were so arranged that they threw the light at the required intervals and blacked it out in between. The lantern of prisms floated round and round the light in a bed of half a ton of mercury and took one minute and forty seconds to complete the circuit, its beam being seen flashing every ten seconds at a distance of seventeen miles in good visibility. It was kept revolving by a clock mechanism underneath, the clock having to be wound up every hour by the keeper on watch. There were 670 prisms in the lantern, weighing three tons in total, the mantle giving a light of about 2,200 candlepower which was magnified by the prisms to 164,000 candlepower.

Observers were often puzzled as to why the light appeared as a beam

The 1904 lighthouse with, in front of it, some railway carriages used as living accommodation in 1929. *Photo: Vera and Ron Pope.*

The bare expanse of the ness to the right of the 1904 lighthouse is now occupied by the nuclear power station. *Photo: Margaret Barnes.*

at regular intervals and not as a continuous light all round. The reason is that the ten lenses were in gunmetal casings or holders and the lens holders formed a ten-sided figure. When the light was operating the ten beams were all showing at once and anyone standing opposite any one of the beams would see it as a direct light. However, as the casing was revolving, ten seconds elapsed before the next facet came into position to repeat the beam and one minute forty seconds before one revolution of the casing was completed.

Below the topmost intermittent white light were fixed red and green lights. These, according to which way they were approached, gave warning of the nearness of the ness, or advised on a safe anchorage. The red light on the east side warned of the dangerous sandbank two and a half miles distant in St Margaret's Bay, while red and green on the west side denoted safe anchorage opposite Rye. These lights were visible for twelve miles.

A navigation aid was the radio beacon that for one minute, every five minutes day and night, sent out in morse the signal DU – dash, dot, dot/ dot, dot, dash. It was effective up to a range of fifty miles and helped ships' radio operators to plot their position. The morse signal DGN – dash, dot, dot/dash, dash, dot/dot – may have also been used. The Dungeness foghorn also sounded in morse, giving three blasts – dot, dash, dot – every two minutes.

The 1904 lighthouse was painted all black to begin with, except for its white lantern housing, but later the tower was black with white bands. It is now all black again so that ships do not confuse it with the black and white 1961 lighthouse. During the Second World War the light was partly covered by a hood to shade it so it could not be seen by the enemy from the sea but was visible by ships from Dover.

At one time wood stays and wire were fixed outward from the balcony rails around the lantern room so night flying birds could alight on them. Later, on advice from the Royal Society for the Protection of Birds, floodlights were directed at the lighthouse so that the birds could see it before they were dazzled by the powerful beam from the light and collided with the tower.

This floodlighting proved to be most effective and was used at other lighthouses. However it was stopped at Dungeness in 1958 when electric light replaced the oil burning lamp. Apparently this did not dazzle the birds so much.

The lighthouse keepers did a watch of four hours at the lantern during the period the light was showing. Should an emergency arise the keeper on duty at the lantern could immediately telephone to the principal keeper in his house or communicate with other keepers nearby. As well as maintaining the light the keepers had other tasks. For the Meteorological Office they did hourly weather reports during the day on wind direction, cloud type, cover and height, visibility, sea temperature and barometric pressure. At night similar reports were prepared at three-hourly intervals.

There was no living accommodation as such in the 1904 tower.

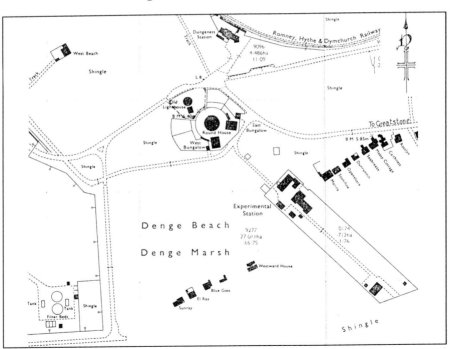

The 1904 lighthouse and its surroundings, from the auction catalogue of 1983.

Keepers lived next door, with their families, in the white painted round house base of the reduced 1792 lighthouse which had been converted for them by Trinity House. When the round house was no longer required it was sold in 1994 by Trinity House and has been converted into flats.

The 1904 lighthouse became redundant in 1961 and it was sold by Trinity House to Gordon Paine of Lydd. After his death in 1982 it was sold the following year by auction and in the particulars of sale was described as:

> 'Brick with outer wall 6ft thick at base both the thickness of the wall and the diameter reducing as it rises to 143 feet in height. . . 169 internal steps curve upwards, hugging the external wall; steps of sandstone except the last section from the service room, which is of steel with a brass handrail. . .on fifth floor is access by low headroom door to external balcony with slate floor and iron railings around the lantern room's circumference.'

The auction catalogue did not mention the view inland to the Kentish Downs and up and down the English Channel, but did add:

> 'Annual rateable value £22. Freehold. No main services.'

The lighthouse is today in private ownership but is open to the public from around Easter to October.

In 1935 an article by C K Lewis in the *Kent County Journal* referred to the local fame achieved by the bees of Dungeness and their honey. He mentions that the wife of the lighthousekeeper, who has an apiary, rarely fails to take prizes in exhibitions for the outstanding quality of her honey.

'Where, in this rather bleak region, do the bees find flowers? ' he asks, and goes on to list those that do exist there as: 'Thrift, sea campion, broom, furze, yellow horned poppy, sea holly, borage, viper's bugloss, and flowers of the blackberry and dewberry.'

In the 1930s one of the principal lighthouse keepers was a Mr Pells. He and his wife lived in a bungalow called The Retreat, between the 1904 lighthouse and the Britannia public house, which is still in existence. Mrs Pells did have numerous hives of bees and it seems likely that she was the prize winning exhibitor.

It was also customary for keepers interested in gardening to cultivate plots close to their living accommodation. They would bring the soil in small quantities to the site, and supplement it with seaweed and whatever else could improve its quality. They would pass the gardens to their replacements when they retired or were relocated to another lighthouse by Trinity House.

At the turn of the century the Ward, Lock and Co guidebooks for Hastings and its vicinity mention the daily steamer trips from Hastings Pier:

> 'From the landing stage the *Brighton Queen, Glen Rosa* and other steamers run during the summer to Folkestone and Dover. Dungeness is some twenty miles away to the east and its revolving light may be seen at night.'

The guide does not say that passengers actually came ashore from the steamers to visit the Dungeness lighthouse – or perhaps to buy the honey. However the shingle beach shelved so steeply into deep water at this point that the steamers were able to venture close inshore so passengers could view the lighthouse and wave to the keepers on duty. In the 1920s and 1930s large cruise liners steamed past so close to the shore that people standing on the beach could clearly hear their dance bands playing. It is possible on these occasions that packages were flung by crew members from the decks of passing ships to those waiting on the shore. Letters for posting perhaps, or a little post blockade smuggling?

The west side of the 1961 lighthouse. Photo: Freda Sexton.

5

The 1961 lighthouse

When the nuclear power station was built near to it the 1904 lighthouse was no longer visible from the south west approaches. Once again Trinity House decided that a new one must be built – the fifth if the two primitive early 'light houses' are included. It was to be unmanned, automatically controlled, and on the site of the 1880 Low Light and fog signal. Responsible for this latest Dungeness lighthouse was Philip Hunt, Trinity House's engineer-in-chief from 1951 to 1967.

Work started in November 1959 and new technical and structural ideas – the results of months of research and testing by Trinity House technicians – were used in co-operation with the architects and engineers of Ronald Ward and Partners.

The slim tower rises to a height of 43 metres from the white concrete base formed by a spiral ramp enclosing the control room with the automatic controls. Its light is at a height of 40 metres above mean high water. The tower is made up of a series of twenty-one pre-stressed concrete drums or rings, each five feet high and twelve feet in diameter, enclosed by a six inch thick wall made of pre-cast concrete at the works of Spun Concrete at Rye and brought to the site on low-loaders. A Coles Conqueror Crane, with a jib 142 feet high and a lifting capacity of 11/ tons, was used to lift each interlocking drum into position. When this operation was complete high tensile steel wires were run down through the drums from the top to the base of the lighthouse and tensioned with powerful jacks before being anchored to concrete blocks to provide the structural strength required to resist the 80mph winds sometimes experienced at Dungeness.

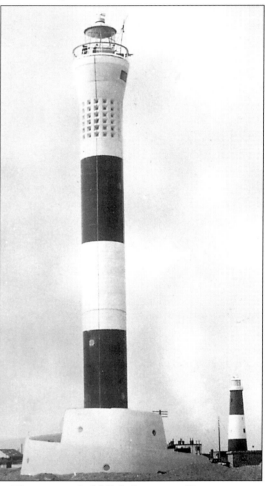

The new and old lighthouses at Dungeness

82

Black and white concrete was used in alternate bands to avoid the necessity of frequent painting. The top band of white is patterned with rows of apertures for the tannoy-type loudspeaker units producing six kilowatts of sound energy which form the electric fog signal. There are sixty units in all, in two banks of thirty, built into the tower itself and facing up and down the English Channel. The signal has a triple frequency sounding three blasts every thirty seconds, its `beam' covering a horizontal arc of about 200 degrees. It is directed out to sea, away from any habitation on shore. Direction finding details are beamed to ships in the Dover Straits by a medium frequency radio beacon which transmits DU in morse every six minutes.

The fog signal is started automatically by a fog detector designed by Trinity House. It consists of a powerful searchlight with a photocell which measures how much light is present. When the visibility falls to two miles the detector switches on the fog signal. A Xenon electric arc lamp with a light of extremely high intensity was tested at Dungeness for the new lighthouse. However, like its predecessor of the 1860s, it also proved difficult to control and was taken out of use, the optic being replaced with a sealed beam unit of a new design by Trinity House engineers.

The Aga Sealed Beam optic comprises four banks of 4x200 watt sealed beam lamps in an aluminium case. It revolves every ten seconds, the beam having an intensity of 1,920,000 candlepower. The lamp gives a white flash every ten seconds and can be seen at a distance of twenty seven miles in clear visibility. A subsidiary fixed sector red and green light in the tower consists of a 500 watt electric filament lamp with 2,500 candlepower and a range of eleven miles in clear visibility. Electricity comes from the National Grid. An auxiliary supply is provided by a six cylinder generator and if that fails there are batteries on which it can operate for up to twenty four hours. There is a computer controlled telephone alarm system to warn of any system failure.

Until 1994, when they were withdrawn by Trinity House, which controls Dungeness from its depot at Harwich, two keepers lived on the site to be on hand should any such failure occur. Now a 'lighthouse caretaker' lives nearby and looks after the cleaning and checking of batteries and bulbs.

The new lighthouse was officially opened by the Duke of Gloucester, a former Master of Trinity House, on June 29, 1960, and came into operation on November 20 the following year, from which date the use of the 1904 lighthouse was discontinued by Trinity House. The 1961 lighthouse, like its predecessor, is floodlit at night to aid migrating birds – in spite of the fact that the area is illuminated by the lights of the nuclear power station.

As part of the opening ceremony a number of plaques were unveiled including an inscribed tablet from the 1792 lighthouse which reads:

'For the direction and comfort of navigators. For the benefit and security of commerce. This lighthouse was erected by Thomas William Coke Esq., of Holkham House in the county of Norfolk, instead of the old [1635] lighthouse which originally stood 540 yards to the northward and which, by means of the land increasing from the violence of the sea, became useless to navigation, AD 1792, the distance from the sea 100 yards at low water'.

BIBLIOGRAPHY

A History of the Marconi Company by W J Baker Methuen 1970

Across the Marshes by Elsie M Jacobs, privately published, Brookland Vicarage 1949

An Old Gate of England by A G Bradley. Robert Scott 1917

Betwixt the Forelands by Clark Russell. Sampson Low 1899

Britannia – Kent (1586) by William Camden, annotated by Gordon J Copley. Hutchinson 1977

British Lighthouses by J P Bowen. British Council/Longmans, Green and Co 1947

Dover Strait Pilot published by the Hydrographer of the Royal Navy 1971

Footpaths of the Kent-Sussex Border by Joseph Braddock. Chaterson Ltd 1947

Goodwin Sands Shipwrecks by Richard Larn. David and Charles 1977

Heroes of the Goodwin Sands by Rev Thomas Treanor. Religious Tract Society 1893

Highways and Byways in Kent by Walter Jerrold. Macmillan 1907

Historic Broadstairs by W H Lapthorne. Thanet Antiquarian Book Club 1980

Kent Railways Remembered by Leslie Oppitz. Countryside Books 1988

Kent Shipwrecks by Alan Bignell. Countryside Books 1991

Lighthouses of England and Wales by Derrick Jackson. David and Charles 1975

Lighthouses, Their Architecture, History and Archeology by Douglas Hague and Rosemarie Christie. Gomer Press 1975

Looming Lights by George Goldsmith Carter. Constable 1945

Marconi Centenaries in 1999 by Gordon Bussey. GEC-Marconi Communications 1999

Memorials of the Goodwin Sands by G Byng Gattie. W H Allen and Co 1890

Official Guide to Romney Marsh Rural District. Century Publications 1964

Smuggling – Flogging Joey's Warriors by John Douch, Crabwell Publications/Buckland Publications 1985

The Bulwark Shore by Caroline Hillier. Eyre Methuen 1980

The Gift from the Sea – Romney Marsh by Anne Roper. Birlings 1984

The Sea, Thine Enemy by Captain Kenneth Langmaid RN. Jarrolds

Wireless at Sea by H E Hancock. Marconi International Marine Communications Co 1950
World's Smallest Public Railway by P Ransome-Wallis. Ian Allen 1964

Fact sheets

Trinity House North Foreland Lighthouse Fact Sheet
Trinity House South Foreland Lighthouse Fact Sheet

Magazine articles

Dungeness Lighthouse. *Illustrated London News,* February 1843
The North Foreland Lighthouse by W H Lapthorne in vol 4 of *Bygone Kent,* 1983
The South Foreland Lighthouse by Lt Col E V Cavenagh
South Foreland History by Ted Powers in *Flash,* the Year Book of Trinity House Services, 1986
The Brake Light Vessel by Anthony Lane in *Bygone Kent,* June 1993
South Foreland. Monograph by Dr Ken Trethaway, 1994

Lightvessel No. 21 East Goodwin.
Photo: Dr. A. R. Lane